Life and Teachings of
LORD JESUS

Sri Swami Sivananda

Published by
THE DIVINE LIFE SOCIETY
P.O. SHIVANANDANAGAR—249 192
Distt. Tehri-Garhwal, Uttarakhand, Himalayas, India
www.sivanandaonline.org, www.dlshq.org

First Edition: 1959
Seventh Edition: 2016
[1,000 Copies]

©The Divine Life Trust Society

ISBN 81-7052-129-7
ES 212

PRICE: ₹ 80/-

Published by Swami Padmanabhananda for
The Divine Life Society, Shivanandanagar, and printed by
him at the Yoga-Vedanta Forest Academy Press,
P.O. Shivanandanagar, Distt. Tehri-Garhwal, Uttarakhand,
Himalayas, India
For online orders and Catalogue visit : dlsbooks.org

PUBLISHERS' NOTE

Sri Swami Sivananda is a cosmic Being. The love of his heart embraces the entire creation. His hands of help and protection reach out to the whole world. His blessings and grace are showered on all alike, irrespective of caste, creed, religion, nationality and sex.

His Ashram on the bank of the Ganga reflects this catholicity of his outlook. In the Ashram are celebrated the festivals of all religions,—the Birthdays of all the Prophets of the world, and the holy days of all creeds.

The Holy Christmas is a very important celebration in the Ashram, observed with as much solemnity and rejoicing as is the Krishna Janmashtami, Ramanavami or the Birthday of Guru Nanakdev.

Christ, the Son of Man, is the Son of God, the Light that is born to save the world of darkness. As the darkness of the world is not an outward phenomenon, so is the remover of darkness not a mere physical personality.

Great men are not seen from their bodies. The great man is the behaviour, the conduct, the character, the speech, the thought and conscious expression of any kind. From these special characteristics the presence of the great man is inferred and directly perceived. He is great who has comprehended that stupendous ocean of Spirit, the Great God that twinkles in all eyes, that resides in the hearts of all beings.

The reverence and esteem in which Lord Jesus is held by Sri Swami Sivananda is well portrayed in this valuable publication from his prolific pen.

—THE DIVINE LIFE SOCIETY

PREFACE

Every year, millions of people all over the world celebrate the Holy Christmas. There are festivities and joyous celebrations, a lot of merry-making. People rejoice that Lord Jesus took birth in our midst about two thousand years ago.

It is certainly an event over which all humanity ought to be proud and jubilant. But it is essential, too, to realise that Lord Jesus had a message to deliver. He laid with his own life and blood, a path for mankind to tread. It is essential that mankind should, in the midst of the joyous celebration of the Holy Event of the Birth of Jesus, reflect on the glorious life of the Lord over His Message. For, in it lies the key to world peace and brotherhood.

May God bless you! May the blessings of Lord Jesus be upon you all.

WHAT CHRISTMAS MEANS TO ME

(Sri Swami Sivananda)

Combining as it does, the joy of life and the Spirit or God, the festival of Christmas comes year after the approaching herald of a new year, with its sweet message and silent shifting of our attention, more and yet more to the spiritual pursuits in which alone consist man's real peace, true progress, and everlasting glory. Whether it was Jane Taylor or Watts who affirmed, "Lord, I ascribe it to Thy grace, and not to chance, as others do, that I was born of Christian race"—it is no expression of any spirit of fanaticism but a humble acknowledgement of the excellent benefits that the genuine Christian way and style of life confers upon one; it is an eloquent tribute to the First Christmas divinely celebrated in the Christ's crib one thousand, five hundred and fifty-six years ago, a tribute paid by one who has reaped in experience the life-making fruits of the seeds sown by the birth of Christ. Besides that elevation of sentiments that inspiration for the inmost spirit in man, that gladness of heart for all, Happy Christmas renews and revivifies in us splendid spiritual values, unyielding spirit of courage, hope, service and sacrifice, a wider and more profound meaning of life to live by. Nothing but a complete volume of weighty writing becomes necessary for any satisfactory narration of the Great Meaning that Christmas has always held for each of us. May this Christrmas bring to every man on earth, immense happiness, persisting peace, a new strength, a long life of service, love, sacrifice and spiritual progress!

....

This message was written in 1956 for including in the special Christmas Issue of 'The Guardian', Madras.

CHILDREN'S SONG

Two little eyes to look to God,
Two little ears to hear to His word,
Two little feet to walk in His ways,
Two little lips to sing His praise,
Two little hands to do His will
And one little heart to love Him still.

CHRISTIAN SERVICE SONGS

1. LEAD KINDLY LIGHT

Lead, kindly Light, amid the encircling gloom
    Lead Thou me on;
The night is dark and I am far from home,
    Lead Thou me on.
Keep Thou my feet, I do not ask to see
The distant scene; one step enough for me.
I was not ever thus, nor prayed that Thou
    Shouldst lead me on;
I loved the garish day, and spite of fears,
Pride ruled my will; remember not past years.
So long Thy power hath blest me, sure it still
    Will lead me on,
O'er moor and fen, o'er crag and torrent, till
    The night is gone,
And with the morn, those angel faces smile,
Which I have loved long since and lost awhile.

2. MAKE ME THINE

Take my life, and let it be
Consecrated, Lord! to Thee;
Take my hands, and let them move
At the impulse of Thy love.
Take my moments and my days,
Let them flow in ceaseless praise.
Take my feet, and let them be
Swift and beautiful for Thee.
Take my voice, and let me sing
Always, only for my King.
Take my lips, and let them be
Filled with messages from Thee.
Take my silver and my gold;
Not a mite would I withhold.

Take my intellect, and use
Every power as Thou shalt choose.
Take my will, and make it Thine;
It shall be no longer mine.
Take my heart; it is Thine own.
It shall be Thy Royal Throne.
Take my love; my Lord, I pour
At Thy feet its treasurestore.
Take myself, and I will be
Ever, only, all for Thee.

3. LOVE SO AMAZING

When I survey the wondrous Cross
On which the Prince of Glory died,
My richest gain I count by loss,
And pour contempt on all my pride.
Forbid it, Lord, that I should boast
Save in the Cross of Christ, my God;
All the vain things that charm me most,
I sacrifice them to His Blood.
See from His Head, His Hands, His Feet,
Sorrow and love flow mingling down;
Did E'er such love and sorrow meet,
Or thorns compose so rich a crown?
Were the whole realm of nature mine,
That were an offering far too small;
Love so amazing, so divine,
Demands my soul, my life, my all,
To Christ, who won for sinners grace
By bitter grief and anguish sore,
Be praise from all the ransomed race,
For ever and for evermore.

4. ROCK OF AGES

Rock of ages, cleft for me,
Let me hide myself in Thee;
Let the Water and the Blood

From Thy river side which flowed,
Be of sin the double cure,
Cleanse me from its guilt and power.
Not the labour of my hands
Can fulfil Thy law's demands;
Could my zeal no respite know.
Could my tears for ever flow,
All for sin could not atone;
Thou must save, and Thou alone.
Nothing in my hand I bring.
Simply to Thy Cross I cling:
Naked, come to Thee for dress,
Helpless, look to Thee for grace;
Foul, I to the Fountain fly;
Wash me, Saviour, or I die.
While I draw this fleeting breath,
When my eyelids close in death,
When I soar through tracts unknown,
See Thee on Thy Judgment Throne;
Rock of ages, cleft for me,
Let me hide myself in Thee.

5. NEARER TO GOD

Nearer, my God, to Thee, nearer to Thee!
E'en though it be a cross that raiseth me,
    Still all my song shall be—
Nearer, my God, to Thee, near to Thee.
Though like the wanderer (the sun gone down)
Darkness be over me—my rest a stone;
    Yet in my dreams I'd be
Nearer, my God, to Thee, nearer to Thee.
Then let the way appear steps unto heaven,
All that Thou sendest me in mercy given;
    Angels to beckon me
Nearer, my God, to Thee, nearer to Thee.

Then with my waking thoughts bright with Thy praise,
Out of my stony griefs Bethel I'll raise;
    So by woes to be
Nearer, my God, to Thee, nearer to Thee.
Or if on joyful wing cleaving the sky,
Sun, moon, and stars forgot, upwards I fly,
Still all my song shall be,
Nearer, my God, to Thee, nearer to Thee.

6. THE MISTS HAVE ROLLED AWAY

When the mists have rolled in splendour
    From the beauty of the hills,
And the sunlight falls in gladness
On the river and the rills.
We recall our Father's promise
    In the rainbow of the spray
We shall know each other better
When the mists have rolled away

CHORUS

We shall know as we are known;
Never more to walk alone,
In the dawning of the morning
Of that bright and happy day;
We shall know each other better
    When the mists have rolled away.
Oft we tread the path before us
    With a weary burdened heart;
Oft we toil amid the shadows
    And our fields are far apart;
But the Saviour's "Come, ye blessed,"
    All our labour will repay,
When we gather in the morning
    Where the mists have rolled away.
We shall come with joy and gladness,
    We shall gather round the Throne;

Face to face with those that love us,
    We shall know as we are known.
And the song of our redemption
    Shall resound through endless day,
When the shadows have departed
    And the mists have rolled away.

7. SILENT NIGHT

Silent night, holy night!
All is calm, all is bright
Round you virgin Mother and Child,
Holy Infant so tender and mild,
Sleep in heavenly peace,
Sleep in heavenly peace.

Silent night, holy night,
Shepherds quake at the sight;
Glories stream from heaven afar,
Heavenly hosts sing alleluia,
Christ, the Saviour, is born!
Christ, the Saviour, is born!

Silent night, holy night,
Son of God, love's pure light
Radiant beams from Thy holy face,
With the dawn of redeeming grace,
Jesus, Lord, at Thy birth,
Jesus, Lord, at Thy birth.

CONTENTS

Publishers' Note	5
Preface	7
What Christmas Means to Me	8
Christian Service Songs	10
Chapter One—LIFE OF LORD JESUS	19

The Message of His Birth—Divine Protection for Baby Jesus—The First Rays of Light—God-Incarnate Seeks a Guru—Temptations and Triumph—The Spiritual Aspect of Jesus's Miracles—Spirit Vs. Form—The Lord's Mission—The Transfiguration—Crusade Against Hypocrisy—The Betrayal—The Holy Supper—The Lord Is Arrested—The Trial and Judgment—Christ on the Cross

Chapter Two—THE BEATITUDES.............. 37

Desirelessness Is Life Divine—Prayer and Yearning for God—Humility: Hallmark of a Hero—Living Monuments of Divine Law—Mercy: A Divine Virtue—Vision of God—Children of God—The Benefactors of Mankind

Chapter Three—THE SERMON ON THE MOUNT .. 43

The Eternal Message of Lord Jesus—Cosmic Love—The Practice of Purity—Divorce Is Undivine—Self-Surrender: Key to Truth—Shun Insincerity—Lord's Prayer—Give Up Fault-finding—The Golden Rule—The Life Divine

Chapter Four—CHRISTMAS MESSAGES OF
          SRI SWAMI SIVANANDA....... 56

Divinise Thy Nature!—Christ: The Prince of Peace—Strain of an Eternal Gospel—The Christ-life Must be Lived—Where Are You, O Saviour?—Awaken Jesus in You and Follow Him—Prayer Is the Answer—The Voice of Jesus—Christ-spirit Must be Acquired

Chapter Five—PARABLES OF LORD JESUS 85

Parable of the Builders—The Good Samaritan—Parable of the Unclean Spirit—The Rich Fool—The Prerequisites—The Pharisee and the Tax Collector—Parable of the Five Foolish Virgins—Parable of the Two Sons—Parable of the Importunate Friend—The Parable of the Sower—Parable of the Lost Sheep—Parable of the Talents—The Parable of the Prodigal Son—Parable of the Hidden Treasure—Parable of the Seed and the Harvest

Chapter Six—A SYMPOSIUM 96

Christmas—Its Spiritual Meaning
—Sri Swami Sivananda............... 96

'Thy Kingdom Come'
—Sri Swami Chidananda............. 100

A Sacramental Life
—Sri Swami Krishnananda............ 105

Christ's Divine Life
—Sri Swami Chidananda............. 110

The Christ to the Spiritual Aspirant
—Sri Swami Krishnananda............ 113

The Promises of Jesus
—Sri Sudarshan Sharma 118

Life of Jesus for a Spiritual Aspirant
—Swami Chidananda................ 121

A Significant Chapter in the Bible
—Sri Swami Sivananda.............. 125

Life and Teachings of
LORD JESUS

Chapter One

LIFE OF LORD JESUS

The Message of His Birth

The Supreme Light descended into this mortal world of gloom and darkness, two thousand years ago.

The Law governing the Lord's descent upon earth is the same at all times, everywhere. When unrighteousness grows and righteousness is waning, when the forces undivine seem to be stronger than the divine forces, when the Word of God or commandments of His Messengers are forgotten or disobeyed, when religious fanaticism follows the letter of the scriptures killing the spirit, it is then that the Lord incarnates Himself on earth, to save Man, to save righteousness. That is why we find so much in common between the birth of Lord Jesus and the Avatara of Lord Sri Krishna.

Even at birth, the Lord had silently begun to deliver His Message. He chose, not a palace but a stable to be His first earthly home. He chose, not royal parents, but humble, poor, but faithful and pious people to own Him, the Lord of the Universe, as their offspring. His scale of values is different from mortal. In His eyes, earthly pomp and splendour, as also pride of piety and vanity of intellect, are not receptacles worthy of His descent: for, "blessed are the pure at heart, for they shall see God."

Mary, the Divine Mother of Lord Jesus, had already been informed by His Angels that the Son of God would be born of her. She married a good man named Joseph, the carpenter. They lived in Nazareth. The ruler of the country in which they lived passed an order that all the people should register their names in their native town or village and then pay tax. Joseph had, therefore, to go to Bethlehem, their native place. However, when they did arrive there, they found that they had virtually no decent house or inn to live in, and had to spend the night in a stable. It was here that the Lord was born.

The blessed, pure and pious shepherds were the next to see the Lord. They were keeping watch over their sheep in the country; and an angel appeared before them and informed them of the Divine Birth. Then the angels sang a beautiful song in praise of the Lord and in so doing, revealed the Purpose of His Descent:

> Glory to God in the highest
> and on earth peace,
> goodwill toward men.

Lord Jesus had come into this world of men in order to re-establish the true and the highest glory of God, peace on earth, and goodwill in the hearts of men towards all fellow-beings. These blessed shepherds were the very first blessed souls on earth to literally worship the Saviour.

Eight days after His Birth, His parents took Him to the temple at Jerusalem for being presented to God, as was the then Jewish custom. A good old man of Jerusalem, named Simeon, was the next to recognise the Divinity of Lord Jesus. When he saw the Lord in the temple, he knew that Jesus was the Saviour, the Divine Light that had descended on earth to dispel the darkness of ignorance and sin, to redeem the people and to lead them along the path of love and goodness, to the realisation of the Kingdom of God within. In the temple that day Anna, a prophetess also saw Lord Jesus and proclaimed that Jesus was the Son of God, who would shine as the Light of the World.

Soon after, the Wise men of the East arrived at Bethlehem to pay their homage to the Lord. When the Lord was born, an exceptionally brilliant star shone upon the sky; and this these wise men knew to be the sure sign that the Messiah promised by earlier Prophets had come. They set out to worship the Messiah. They followed the direction of the star and came to the kingdom of Herod. They explained their mission to King Herod whom their tale frightened, more than it pleased; and Herod requested them to let him, too, know of the whereabouts of the Divine Child, to enable him, as he said, to worship Him, though in his heart of hearts he desired to do away with the child. The wise men continued to pursue the Star which shone above the house of the Lord. They recognised the Divine Babe, fell on their knees and worshipped Him and offered Him costly presents, as a humble token of their devotion and reverence.

Divine Protection for Baby Jesus

Angels warned them not to reveal Jesus's whereabouts to Herod and so the wise men went their way without meeting Herod once again. Herod, thus, frustrated in his nefarious ambition, ordered that all children in Bethlehem below the age of two should be mercilessly killed. The King's officers readily carried out his orders; and thousands of little babes were quickly despatched to the Lotus-Feet of the Lord, in Heaven.

But Joseph and Mary, along with Lord Jesus, had been forewarned by angels of the coming danger, and they had escaped into Egypt over which Herod had no authority. The Lord remained in Egypt for some time, till the angels once again appeared before them and announced the death of King Herod. Though Joseph, Mary and Jesus returned to their native country, they chose to proceed to Nazareth, as Joseph felt life was not safe near King Herod's son who ruled in Judea.

At Nazareth, Lord Jesus, the Son of God, the Incarnation of His Light, the Saviour, grew up as a dutiful son of the pious parents and learnt carpentry form Joseph. The Divine Master who latter in life was to shape the twelve great apostles, and whose flaming words were to shape for all time to come the destinies of countless human beings and even nations upon earth,—He busied Himself in learning carpentry, shaping tools and furniture from raw wood.

The First Rays of Light

When the Lord was twelve years old, Joseph and Mary took Him to Jerusalem for the Feast of the Passover. Jesus was very much interested in the Temple and the discourses of the priests there. In fact, He was so much engrossed in the thoughts of God and His Divine Law, that when His parents had left the temple and were returning to Nazareth, He returned to the temple and joined a group of religious teachers who were discussing religious questions. Even to these masters of philosophy, His words were astounding.

Soon Joseph and Mary discovered that Jesus was not following them. In great consternation they returned to the temple and found Him there. Mary gently chided Him for thus slipping away from them to which the Lord replied in those wonderful mystic words: "Did you not know that I must be about My Father's business?" The fond parents were only even more puzzled.

For about fourteen years thereafter, Jesus spent His life in India and lived like a Hindu or a Buddhist monk. He had burning dispassion and the spirit of renunciation. In India he assimilated Hindu ideals and principles. Some Christians do not believe in this account of the Lord's "missing period." They argue it is not specifically mentioned in the Bible.

In matters connected with persons who lived as far back as nearly twenty centuries ago, there is bound to be slight divergences of view. The Old Testament naturally cannot contain any reference. The New Testament consists of Gospels, etc., written by His Disciples, after He was enlightened. It is obviously futile to search for a reference about the period preceding this,—which was the period during which he travelled in India where He got initiation from sages and seers—in accounts of His actions written by people who could never have had any knowledge of His earlier days. It has been the belief of many historians that at some time during the missing period Jesus travelled in India. Anyway there is nothing untenable in this view, and its acceptance would only strengthen the bonds of love between the East and the West, and promote good will between the two hemispheres, which is the Mission of the Lord.

God-Incarnate Seeks a Guru

John the Baptist, son of the priest Zacharias and his wife Elizabeth, had, in accordance with angel Gabriel's prophecy begun to baptize people and to prepare them to receive the Light of the Lord Jesus. Lord Jesus was now about thirty years of age, and sought John to be baptized by him on the banks of the river Jordan. John recognised Jesus's Divinity and asked: "Dost Thou come to me, when I have need to be baptized by Thee?" But the Lord had determined to set an example to mankind: spiritual illumination can be had through a Guru (Preceptor). The moment the baptism was complete, Lord Jesus saw a vision of God's spirit descending like a dove and alighting upon Him, and He heard a heavenly voice say: "Thou art my beloved son, I am well pleased with thee."

Even John the Baptist had often declared that Lord Jesus was greater than he. But look at the Lord's devotion to His Preceptor! He said: "Of those born of women there has not arisen one greater than John the Baptist." Devotion to the Guru (Preceptor) is the key that unlocks the realms divine: and even the Supreme Being, the Mass of Supreme Consciousness, when He descends upon this earth, sets a great example in Guru-Bhakti.

Temptations and Triumph

After the baptism, Lord Jesus resorted to seclusion in the wilderness and practised extreme austerities and fasted. At the end of 40 days of such fasting He was hungry. Austerities and meditation had, no doubt, earned for Him divine powers to work miracles. And, the Lord did perform miracles to save people and to heal them. "Why not use those powers now, convert stones into bread, and appease your hunger," tempted Satan, the Evil One. But, Lord Jesus resolutely refused to yield to this temptation, saying: "Man shall not live by bread alone, but by every word that proceeds out of the Mouth of God." Then, again, the temptation arose to test the miraculous powers; "Why not throw yourself from a high tower of the temple; if you are God's Son, angels shall bear Thee up," whispered Satan, the Evil One. But once again Lord Jesus brushed the tempter aside, saying: "Thou shalt not tempt the Lord thy God." A third temptation was placed before Him, when the Evil One took Him to the top of a high mountain, showed Him the world, and said: "All these will I give Thee, if Thou wilt fall down and worship me." But, will Lord Jesus agree? No. He grew stern and rebuked: "Get thee hence, Satan; for it is written in the Scriptures, 'Thou shalt worship the Lord thy God and Him only shalt thou serve'." The Evil One disappeared and the angels ministered to the Lord.

In this great incident of His Life, the Lord had not only given us three most inspiring pieces of instruction, but had also warned by his own example that psychic powers are to be considered as obstacles on his path by the true spiritual aspirant, and that even if, by His Grace, these powers do come to him, he should never even think of utilizing them for his selfish ends. Even when his life was at stake, Lord Jesus would not use His miraculous powers to prevent His being crucified. All the miracles He performed during His travels were prompted by the supreme compassion of His heart which overflowed with love and mercy towards all beings. He healed the sick and even raised the dead. But what He really did was to cast out the devils from the persons whom He healed. Their past evil deeds and their hidden evil tendencies had taken the form of their physical and mental ailments. Jesus reclaimed the lost souls and restored to them their pristine purity: He obtained for them, the Lord's Mercy and Pardon. In his radiant Presence, they not only had great faith in God, but they felt a real eagerness to follow Lord Jesus and lead a new, divine life in accordance with His instructions. It was this faith and this true repentance—repentance that was at once translated into a complete self-reformation—that drew forth from Lord Jesus, His compassionate Healing Grace.

The Spiritual Aspect of Jesus's Miracles

Jesus, after the period of His seclusion and austerities, came back to His native village, eager to impart His wisdom to His fellow-men. John the Baptist had already declared to the people that the Kingdom of God was at hand and called upon people to repent with a contrite heart and effect a change of heart in themselves in order to be able to enter the Kingdom of God. Jesus, too, began with a repetition of this Message. But, whereas John had painted God as a stern Judge, Lord Jesus spoke of Him as the All-Merciful Father Who loved to save the sinner. To Lord Jesus, faith in God, earnestness in prayer, and ethical discipline ranked far above religious observances and ceremonies. This made Him the friend of the oppressed and repressed sections of the people and those whom the orthodox church had excommunicated. Jesus welcomed them all, forgave their sins, and blessed them. "Come unto me all ye that labour and are heavy-laden and I will give you rest," said He; and thousands sought Him and found peace and solace at His feet. One of His chosen twelve disciples was a publican, rejected and despised by the orthodox Jews. And one of the greatest and closest of his followers was Mary Magdalene who was so sinful that it is said, Lord Jesus cast out seven devils from her.

One day as Lord Jesus was passing by, a crowd had collected around a woman who had been charged with adultery and had been sentenced "to be stoned to death." As the crowd was about to carry out this execution, Lord Jesus came upon the scene. Such was the magnetic and divine personality that He possessed that the people instinctively obeyed His command to desist from the cruel act. When He had heard their story of the woman's "unpardonable" sin, He quietly said: "Let him that is without sin among you, cast the first stone on her." This powerful utterance of the Lord at once turned the gaze of each one there within himself. Who could be without sin? Introspection revealed their own defects. One by one, the people hung their heads down and left the place. "Where are they," Lord Jesus asked the woman, "did no man condemn thee?" "No, my Lord," said she. "Neither do I condemn thee; go thy way and sin no more," said the Lord summing up in this beautiful incident the very essence of His Divine Message.

On another occasion, when a devotee, bathed Lord Jesus' feet with her tears, wiping them with her hairs and applying precious ointment over them, the Lord blessed her and granted her forgiveness for all her sins. This enraged some of the people, who questioned His right to grant forgiveness for sins.

Spirit Vs. Form

By now the first disciples had gathered around Lord Jesus. The Pharisees on one occasion found Jesus's disciples plucking corn on Sabbath Day and eating it. When this was brought to the notice of the Lord, He said: "The Sabbath was made for man and not man for the Sabbath; so that the Son of Man is lord even of the Sabbath." This greatly displeased the Pharisees who waited for another opportunity.

While Jesus was teaching in a synagogue on a Sabbath Day the Pharisees brought to him a sick man, wishing to find out if he would heal him on the Sabbath Day. Jesus turned upon them and asked: "Is it right to do good, or evil, on Sabbath Day?" They were unable to answer. Jesus turned to the sick man and healed him. This had conclusively set the Pharisees against Him.

Jesus had gone to Jerusalem to attend the Feast of the Passover and Nicodemus, one of the chief Pharisees, met the Lord at night. Though Nicodemus acknowledged Jesus to be a teacher who had come from God, he said: "I am not able to understand and appreciate all that you teach." To this the Lord replied in words pregnant with deep spiritual import: "A man must be born again if he is to see the Kingdom of God—reborn not of the body, but in the spiritual sense." Lord Jesus proclaimed that a true change of heart constituted this rebirth.

On his way back to Galilee from Jerusalem, Jesus passed through Samaria. At Sychar He took rest near a well, while His disciples had gone into the town to buy food. A Samaritan woman came to the well to fetch water; and the Lord asked her to give Him some water to drink. She hesitated as no Jew could have anything to do with Samaritans. The Lord then told her of her past life. At once she understood that Lord Jesus was a Prophet; and He, too, admitted that He was the Messiah. The surprised woman at once spread the news to all the people of the city and they gathered around him, proclaiming: "This is truly the Christ, the Saviour of the world."

When Lord Jesus had returned to Cana, a nobleman approached Him and prayed to Him for His Healing Grace upon his boy who was lying dangerously ill at Capernaum. The Lord replied: "Go your way, for your son will live." At the very moment the Lord uttered these words, the boy had regained his health. Even as the nobleman returned to Capernaum, his servants greeted him with this happy news.

The Lord's Mission

On one Sabbath Day at Nazareth, Lord Jesus claimed for Himself the fulfilment of the prophecy of Isaiah: "The spirit of the Lord is upon Me because he has anointed Me to preach, to heal and to set at liberty." This greatly enraged the congregation at the synagogue. Though the Lord had been recognised as the Son of God, as a Prophet, and as the Light of the World by others, to the people of Nazareth, Jesus was but the son of a carpenter! These unfortunate people drove Jesus out of Nazareth. Said the Lord: "In his own country, a prophet has no honour."

Jesus then went over to Capernaum, along with His disciples. Crowds of people gathered around Him wherever He went; and He preached Real Religion to all of them. One day He saw Andrew and Peter cleaning their fishing nets. As usual a crowd had gathered around Him; and thus, sitting in Peter's boat, Lord Jesus preached His Gospel to the crowd. Then, He asked Peter to launch out into the deep and let down the nets. Peter had not much of a hope of catching any fish; but he obeyed the Lord. He caught such a lot of fish that he had to get the assistance of several other comrades, to drag the net up. Turning to them, Lord Jesus said: "Follow Me and I will make you fishers of men." They followed Him implicitly and became His chosen disciples.

His relatives had heard of His attitude and the strange gospel He preached, and also discovered that He was thus incurring the displeasure of the powers-that-be. They thought that He was beside Himself and wanted to persuade Him to give up this opposition to constituted authority. While He was preaching on the lakeside at Capernaum, His brothers and His mother went over there to meet Him. When He was told of their arrival there, He asked, "Who is my mother and my brethren?" and answered it Himself: "Behold my mother and my brethren," pointing to those who sat around him; "for, whosoever shall do the will of God, the same is my brother and sister and mother,"—thus granting the closest relationship with Him to all mankind for all time to come.

Jesus's fame as the divine healer spread far and wide; and people came to Him from far and near to be healed of various ailments. One day, as He was preaching at a synagogue in Capernaum, a man who had a fit of madness was brought to Him. Jesus rebuked the spirit of madness that possessed him and said, "Silence! Come out of him." The man was healed.

Similarly Peter's mother-in-law was cured of a serious fever; and hundreds of others were healed by a mere touch of His Hand.

One day, seeing the vast multitude follow Him, He went up a hill and preached His famous *"Sermon on the Mount."*

As He came down the mountain, a leper approached Him and prayed to Him for His Healing Grace. By a mere touch Lord Jesus cured him. A centurion approached Him and said that his servant was sick at home. Though Lord Jesus promised to go to the centurion's house, the latter prayed sincerely that He need not and that His mere wish would heal the ailing servant at home. Lord Jesus admired his faith and remarked: "I have not found so great faith, no, not in Israel." He blessed the servant and, though he was physically far away, the servant was instantly healed.

Seeing the multitudes following Him wherever He went, Lord Jesus wanted to sail to the country of the Gergensenes. As he boarded the ship, a scribe wanted to go with Him. Lord Jesus turned to him and said: "The foxes have holes, and the birds of the air have nests; but the Son of Man hath nowhere to lay his head." The Great Lord had no home of His own; but today every human heart is His Abode—such is the glorious fruit of renunciation. He who would follow Him should similarly give up all attachment to the things of the world and renouncing all that is worldly, attain to Freedom.

Another, a disciple, wanted leave to bury his dead father. To him, the Lord said: "Follow me, let the dead bury their dead." That is His stirring call. "Follow Me," says He. Bestow no thought on the meaningless concerns of the world where people who are dead to an understanding of their real nature weep over the death of and bury those who are dead to the world. He who is alive to his real duty will follow Him.

And they got into the boat and sailed away. At night, a violent tempest raged over the sea and the boat was tossed over angry waves. The disciples were concerned lest the boat should capsize. They went to the Lord and woke Him up. He smiled at their lack of faith—how could the boat with Him on board capsize?—and commanded the tempest to stop. All was quiet immediately; and this greatly increased the faith of the disciples in Him—"What manner of man is this, that even the winds and the sea obey him!" said they to one another.

When He returned to His own city once again, the people brought to him a man afflicted with palsy. The Lord pronounced His blessing upon him, saying: "Son, be of good cheer; thy sins be forgiven thee." "This is blasphemy," cried the scribes. But the Lord reaffirmed that He had the power on earth to forgive the sins of men and commanded the sick man to get up and walk home. Lo, the miracle happened and the man was healed.

Lord Jesus would frequently dine with the Pharisees as well as those whom the public regarded as sinners. The orthodox men of religion could not understand Him. He dispelled their doubts by His bold declaration: "They that be whole need not a physician, but they that are sick. I will have mercy, and not sacrifice; for I am not come to call the righteous, but sinners to repentance."

One day, a King came to the Lord and said to Him: "My daughter is dead; but I have the faith that if You come and touch her, she will live again." The Lord followed the ruler to his house; and another supreme miracle of faith took place on the way. A poor woman sorely afflicted with a disease which made her bleed profusely merely touched His garment as He walked along: and she was instantly healed. Later, when the Lord touched the King's daughter, she rose and came back to life.

Thus wherever He went, the Lord healed the sick, made the blind men see and deaf men hear again.

John the Baptist was assassinated. When Lord Jesus heard of it He boarded a ship and went to a desert. A crowd followed Him there, too. When evening came, the disciples found that they had only five loaves of bread and two fish; and there were about five thousand men and their families to partake of these! But, Lord Jesus offered a prayer to Heaven and broke the loaves and gave them all.

He asked His disciples to sail away from there and He Himself went into seclusion to pray. At the dead of night the disciples who were in the boat which had gone away from the shore watched with amazement Jesus walking over the water towards them. They even thought it was a spirit. Peter said to the Lord: "If it is You, Lord, then make me also walk over the water." Jesus said: "Come," and Peter was able to walk over the sea. But on the way, Peter was frightened by the wind, and his faith shook; and he at once began to sink. Jesus held out His hand, saved him and said: "Oh ye of little faith, wherefore didst thou doubt?" He who had faith in the Lord could accomplish anything on earth.

A rich young ruler one day approached the Lord and asked: "Good Master, what should I do to inherit eternal life?" Lord Jesus replied: "You should keep the Commandments." "Oh yes," the young ruler replied: "and I have kept them since my childhood. What else should I do?" "There is one thing more," said Jesus, "and that is: sell all that you have and give to the poor. Then take up your Cross and follow me." At the very mention of this sacrifice and renunciation, the young ruler turned away and walked off. Lord Jesus remarked: "It is easier for a camel to enter the eye of a needle than for a rich man to enter the Kingdom of God."

The Transfiguration

One day Lord Jesus took Peter, James and John, to a mountain retreat. Suddenly Lord Jesus stood transfigured above them. His face shone like Sun and His clothes were lustrous, too. With Him were Moses and Elias. A bright cloud overshadowed them, and a voice said: "This is my beloved Son, in whom I am well pleased: hear ye him." The disciples were afraid and fell down. Lord Jesus came near them and touched them, and said: "Arise, be not afraid". When they raised their head, they saw only Lord Jesus and marvelled at the Vision they had of Him.

Jesus thus taught many a great lesson to His disciples and others; and He spoke boldly and authoritatively on ethics and revealed spiritual truths through parables.

Crusade Against Hypocrisy

Then one day He went over to Jerusalem. In the temple there he drove away all those who carried on business transactions—purchasing and selling worldly goods, and reminded them: "It is written—My House shall be called the house of prayer; but ye have made it a den of thieves." Seeing His wonderful miraculous powers to heal, the people hailed Him as

"The Son of David;" and this irritated the priests. They assailed Him with numerous questions to which Jesus replied in a manner that caused wonderment and jealousy. But the priests could do no harm to Him, as they were afraid of public reaction, as He was regarded as a Prophet by the people.

In unmistakable terms He denounced the Pharisees and scribes. He said, "Woe unto you, scribes and Pharisees, hypocrites! for ye are like unto whited sepulchres, which indeed appear beautiful outward, but are within full of dead men's bones and of all uncleanness. Even so ye also outwardly appeal righteous unto men, but within ye are full of hypocrisy and inequity."

Jesus's teachings had greatly angered these hypocrites and they were conspiring to put an end to His life. He too, during the last days of His sojourn upon this earth frequently predicted that He would be crucified. When Lord Jesus was in Bethany, one day a woman-devotee came to Him and with great faith and devotion anointed Him with a very costly ointment. Even the Lord's disciples felt it was a waste and remarked that she could as well have sold it and served the poor with the money. But Jesus who understood her heart, and the coming events too, remarked: "Why trouble ye the woman for she hath wrought a good work upon me. For ye have the poor always with you; but me ye have not always. For in that she hath poured this ointment on my body, she did it for my burial."

The Betrayal

Now a strange thing happened. If it was inevitable, nevertheless it was disgraceful. One of His own disciples betrayed the Lord. Even as the Lord Himself said during the Last Supper, "Woe unto that man by whom the Son of Man is betrayed; it had been good for that man if he had not been born." As the Pharisees were conspiring to do away with the Lord, Judas Iscariot went to the chief priests and offered to betray the Lord for a petty sum of thirty pieces of silver.

The feast of the Passover was approaching. As commanded by the Lord, the disciples prepared for the feast in a pious citizen's house. Strangely enough, as soon as they were also seated and had begun to eat, Lord Jesus let fall a remark: "Verily I say unto you, that one of you shall betray me." There was great consternation in the hearts of all. He even gave a hint that He knew who it would be, by explaining it: "He that dippeth his hand with me in the dish, the same shall betray me." But perhaps they did not notice whom He meant.

The Holy Supper

During this Holy Supper, the Lord took a bread, broke it and distributed it among his disciples saying: "This is my body"; and gave them wine with the significant remark: "This is my blood of the new testament, which is shed for many for the remission of sins." Yes, the All-Merciful Lord Jesus lived and died so that the sins of mankind might be forgiven and that men might learn to repent truly and lead the life divine thereafter.

When the Holy Supper was over, the Lord knelt down at the feet of each one of His disciples and washed his feet. To the amazed disciples, He said: "If I then, your Lord, and Master, have washed your feet, ye also ought to wash one another's feet."

When they were all going over to the Mount of Olives the Lord gave a broad hint of the events that soon followed. Peter affirmed His devotion to the Lord to which the Lord replied: "This night before the cock crows, thou shalt deny me thrice." They were all puzzled.

The Lord Is Arrested

Then they came to a place called Gethesemane. Lord Jesus wanted to seclude Himself for a while and pray to the Divine Father. He prays. He knows that the end has come. He prays: "O my Father, if this cup may not pass away from me, except I drink it, thy will be done." The three disciples that He had taken with Him to this secluded spot, are unable even to keep vigil and this evokes from the Lord the remark: "The spirit indeed is willing, but the flesh is weak." Thrice he prayed to the Lord on this fateful night.

He called His disciples to go; but instantly He was surrounded by a multitude of people, headed by the chief priests, armed with various weapons. Judas had told the priests that in order to point out to them who was Lord Jesus he would kiss Him. Judas came right up to Lord Jesus and as if out of devotion, kissed Him. This was the signal for the people to arrest the Lord.

One of the Lord's disciples, wishing to defend the Lord, drew a sword and struck off the ear of a servant of the priests. And this drew from the Lord the memorable words: "Put up again the sword into its place; for all they that take the sword shall perish with the sword,"—a maxim which the rulers of all nations would do well to remember.

The Lord is unwilling even to pray to the Divine Father for miraculous help on this occasion: for His Will be done. The Lord had to be crucified so that for all time to come the Cross shall stand as the Holiest Symbol of Sacrifice and Love.

The Trial and Judgment

A mock trial was held before the high priest Caiaphas where the Lord was charged with blasphemy. The high priest said: "I abjure thee by the living God, that thou tell us whether thou be the Christ, the Son of God." Lord Jesus replied: "Thou hast said: nevertheless I say unto you. Hereafter shall ye see the Son of man sitting on the right hand of power and coming in the clouds of heaven." The priests sentenced Him to death for this blasphemy.

At the same time Peter, outside, was asked if he was a disciple of Lord Jesus: and, out of fright, he denied it! The cock crew after the third denial; and suddenly realising his mistake, Peter went out and cried bitterly.

Lord Jesus was then taken before the governor Pontius Pilate.

In the meantime, Judas who had realised the blunder he had committed went over the priests and threw the silver pieces before them and said: "I have sinned in that I have betrayed the innocent blood." But it was too late! He ran outside and hanged himself.

Christ on the Cross

The trial before Pilate was very much like the previous one. The priests and elders had many charges against the Lord. They all cried again and again, "Let him be crucified." But Pilate's wife had strange dreams and felt her husband should not shed the blood of the innocent Lord Jesus. She told him so. When Pilate found it was inevitable, he took water and washed his hands of this terrible sin. He had tried his best to release the Lord, finding Him innocent. But the priests and others had their way. When He was condemned to death on the Cross, He was taken to a place called Golgotha. A crown of thorns had been placed upon his head.

At Golgotha they had Him crucified. The Lord said: "Father, forgive them, for they know not what they do." Pilate had the accusation written over His head: "This is Jesus the King of the Jews." Many were the people that mocked at Him. But He was unmoved. By the side of the Cross were Jesus's mother, and his mother's sister, Mary the wife of Cleophas, and Mary Magdalene. After a while Lord Jesus cried: "I thirst;" and the guards gave him a little vinegar. At last He cried: "Father, into thy hands I commend my spirit," and saying so, He gave up the ghost.

There was a big earthquake. The graves were opened and the bodies of saints which lay there arose. Many people had visions of these holy saints. A rich man named Joseph asked the Pilate to give him Jesus's body. The body was entombed in a sepulchre which was securely sealed with a big stone.

On the third day, there was a great earthquake. An angel from Heaven had opened the sepulchre. The keepers of the sepulchre and the women—Mary Magdalene and the other Mary—were all frightened. The angel told them that the Lord had risen, and that they would see Him in Galilee!

Before these women could tell the disciples, the latter had met Jesus who said to them: "All Hail." The disciples went to a mountain in Galilee and worshipped Him. The Lord gave them His last Message:

"Go ye therefore and teach all nations, baptizing them in the name of the Father, and of the Son, and of the Holy Ghost; teaching them to observe all things whatever I have commanded you; and lo, I am with you Always, even unto the end of the world."

May Lord Jesus ever thus dwell in your heart, bringing Light and Love, into your Life! Amen.

Chapter Two
THE BEATITUDES

What is blessedness?

God has indeed blessed everyone. The human birth is a great blessing conferred upon you by the Lord. Intelligence and the power of discrimination are further blessings which He has conferred upon you. In everyday language we hear it said that such and such a person had been blessed with a child or some such material advantage.

True, but the blessedness which Lord Jesus refers to at the very commencement of His Divine Sermon on the Mount, is something different. It is real blessedness. It is a condition in which the Spirit of God enters the heart of man, and when man is no longer of the world but is transformed into a divine being. The spiritual aspirant has been accepted by God as His own: that is real blessedness. The individuality ceases, and the glorious saint becomes as it were, an instrument of His Hands—nay, almost a part of His Being, carrying out His Will, living a Divine Life, representing Him on this earth. That is true blessedness. One who has attained to this blessedness is a blessing for humanity.

Who are the blessed?

Desirelessness Is Life Divine

Blessed are the poor in spirit; for theirs is the Kingdom of Heaven. Poor in spirit are they that have emptied themselves of all ego. "Spirited" men proud of their wealth, proud of their pedigree, proud of their learning, and proud of their wisdom have no place in the Kingdom of Heaven. What they seek truly and sincerely they shall get. But, what do they seek? They strive to get the admiration of men, popularity in the world and prosperity in terms of worldly goods. That they may get: though the fleeting nature of things mundane is sure to make them feel miserable eventually. But they that are poor in spirit, desire nothing for themselves in this world. Poverty-stricken desire dies a silent death, within them. Wisdom they have in abundance. But it has become so integrally a part of their being that they are not aware of it! When brought to their notice, they ascribe it to the Lord. They own nothing; they have nothing; they want nothing; they themselves do not exist as independent entities—they are His. Therefore He *lives* in them; and His Grace flows through them. "*Theirs* is the Kingdom of Heaven." What a grand reward they get from renouncing the things of this world of pain and death! The Kingdom of Heaven belongs to them. They are the owners, the rulers of the Kingdom of Heaven. Through them humanity could attain salvation.

Prayer and Yearning for God

Blessed are they that mourn; for they shall be comforted. The great devotee of the Lord mourns on account of separation from Him. The zealous seeker after God mourns because lurking human weaknesses impede his attainment of perfection. This is not mourning in the usual sense of the term; there is no weeping and wailing. There is a strange joy in his mourning. There is a great yearning; there arises a powerful and sincere prayer from the bottom of the heart. It is a prayer for His Grace, for the enlightenment of the heart of human beings, and for His Redeeming Wisdom to fill the soul of every human being on earth. For, remember, the Blessed One has no possessions and has no desire; what will he mourn for? His mourning is truly a yearning; not that he wishes to achieve anything for himself, but that mankind might be blessed. "They shall be comforted": surely, it is because these blessed ones are comforted again and again that there is prosperity in the world and, in spite of so much unrighteousness, there continue to be a number of seekers after Truth, generation after generation. This is the comfort they pray for; and it is granted by the Lord. Therefore are they truly God's blessings on humanity.

Humility: Hallmark of a Hero

Blessed are the meek; for they shall inherit the earth. Meekness is not weakness. Humility is the hallmark of the hero. The first beatitude promised the Kingdom of Heaven to the egoless saint; now, this beatitude proclaims that the meek shall inherit the earth. He who humbly serves God and humanity; he who humbly submits to His Will and accepts everything that comes as His Grace; he who is truly humble at heart, realising His Omnipotent, Omniscient, Omnipresence—such a blessed one radiates blessedness. The whole world is drawn to him; for in his very presence people feel an inexpressible peace and bliss. He has no need for the earthly kingdoms nor for the things of this earth. But he rules the hearts of all human beings—even as Lord Jesus rules the hearts of the entire humanity today.

Living Monuments of Divine Law

Blessed are they which do hunger and thirst after righteousness; for they shall be filled. The significance is perfectly clear. But an implication is worth noting. Righteousness which is God's Will is omnipresent. God's Grace is ever ready to fill man's heart, and make him subserve His Will, thus exalting himself. But it is the egoistic self-willed man who denies Its entry into his heart. To obtain His Grace, to let His Will be done through your being, to let His Righteousness permeate your personality, is, therefore, much easier than you imagine. You have to hunger after it; you have to yearn for it. You have to evince a keen desire to become divine. You have to aspire to lead a righteous life. You have to pray to Him to fill you with Grace. This aspiration, this prayer, opens the inner gate to the chamber of your soul and it is at once flooded with His Grace. Truly blessed are they that are thus filled. For filled with His Righteousness, they will live and move about as living monuments of the Divine Law, thus inspiring others, too, to exalt themselves and transform the very earth into paradise.

Mercy: A Divine Virtue

Blessed are the merciful; for they shall obtain mercy. God is all-mercy. The life-giving warmth of the sun, the life-sustaining purity of fresh air, the sparkling water which quenches your thirst and makes life possible, the good earth that yields nourishing food, besides providing you with a place to dwell—these constantly remind you that God is all-mercy. In order that you might evolve, He has given you a human birth and placed you in circumstances best suited to your temperament and calculated to accelerate your progress towards perfection. He gives you opportunities galore to exercise the divine qualities that are latent in you so that you can become perfect, even as He is Perfect. The beggar at your door; the orphan on the road; the naked, the unlettered, the hungry and the diseased children of God—they are there to provide you chances to exercise the divine mercy in you. Open your eyes and serve them. Clothe the naked; educate the unlettered; feed the hungry and heal the diseased ones. Thus would you grow in mercy. For, God is all-mercy. When you are merciful, you will obtain His Mercy. When you have His mercy, you are blessed indeed; and you are a blessing to mankind, for, everyone who comes in contact with you will witness the miracle of His Mercy, healing, consoling, enlightening everyone and filling the world with the light of wisdom, peace and bliss.

Vision of God

Blessed are the pure at heart; for they shall see God. You do not have to travel to distant lands to see God. You do not have to wait till you shed this human body and ascend to heaven in order to see God. Here and now you can see Him. And, there is only one condition prerequisite—purity of heart. The heart should be washed of all impurities—lust, anger, greed, egoism, and a host of other evils that have made your heart their home.

God is seated in your heart. But the veil of impurity hides Him from your vision. All that you have to do is to remove this veil, cast off this impurity from your heart. And you will behold Him here and now in all His Glory and in all His Splendour.

Blessed are they that thus have a vision of God. For they shall radiate His Blessings to the whole world.

Children of God

Blessed are the peacemakers; for they shall be called the children of God. God created the world. He is the Father of all creation. All beings on earth are His children. The entire mankind is but one family. He who quarrels with another, he who promotes wars and disharmony between communities and nations, works contrary to this Divine Law of Unity. Whereas he who brings people together in love and harmony, who strives to establish peace on earth, and harmony among human hearts—he works in unison with the Divine Law. He is therefore worthy of being called a real child of God. For, he has inherited the divine qualities of the Lord in the fullest measure.

First find the peace within thy own heart through prayer and humility. See God first and you will share His Peace. Then radiate peace to humanity. Your very presence will make for peace. You will radiate Peace. Blessed are such peacemakers for they are a boon to this world torn with strifes and wars.

The Benefactors of Mankind

Blessed are they which are persecuted for righteousness' sake; for theirs is the Kingdom of Heaven.

Blessed are ye, when men shall revile you and persecute you, and shall say all manner of evil against you falsely, for my sake.

Rejoice, and be exceeding glad: for great is your reward in Heaven! for so persecuted they the prophets which were before you.

Saints are a blessing to humanity. They are the greatest benefactors of mankind. There is even this much of peace and happiness in the world only because time and again the glorious saints and men-of-God have been born here on earth and re-established His righteousness on earth.

Yet, such is the tragedy of the world we live in, that these men of God are revolted against, vilified and crucified by a section of the humanity. The followers of the philosophy of the flesh, the worms that wallow in worldliness, the sensuous and senseless sons of Satan,—cannot "endure" the Divine Radiance of the godly saints, even as the owl cannot endure the brilliant light of the day. Yet, such is the divine nature of these blessed saints that they are "unable" even to resist the evil, retaliate or even protect themselves from the onslaughts of the evil-minded. The history of the world is witness to numberless persecutions in which the blessed ones have laid down their lives, in an endeavour to uphold righteousness.

And, the marvel of marvels! By thus sacrificing their life to the great divine cause of righteousness, "for His sake," they have fulfilled their mission. The supreme sacrifice of their life itself is the crowning glory of their mission. The one event of self-sacrifice affects Human Mind more profoundly than all the preaching could have done; and people begin to realise that if this great and blessed man could sacrifice his very life to the principle he upheld during his lifetime, it was well worth their adherence. A near-revolution takes place in the heart of man and penitently he takes to the path of righteousness, leaving once for all the path of evil on which the life-blood of their Beloved One, the Glorious Man-of-God, was shed.

In life as well as in giving it up the saint fulfils the one great mission of re-establishing righteousness on earth. That is God's Mission. He who makes it his own is truly blessed. And, he is a blessing unto all mankind for he shows the way to God, to the fountain-source of life, light and love; of peace, plenty and prosperity.

May the choicest blessings of the Blessed Ones be upon you all! May you all become truly blessed in this very birth!

Chapter Three

THE SERMON ON THE MOUNT

The Eternal Message of Lord Jesus

"Whosoever heareth these sayings of mine, and doeth them, I will liken him unto a wise man, which built his house upon a rock. And everyone that heareth these sayings and doeth them not shall be likened unto a foolish man which built his house upon the sand," said the Lord at the conclusion of the famous Sermon on the Mount. The Sermon was not a philosophical discussion to be listened to and understood, perhaps, and forgotten later. In that glorious Sermon He had breathed the spirit of God. The Sermon was the word of God, the Eternal Message that is ever afire with the flame of Divinity. Jesus lives in that Sermon.

Remember, the angels had commanded Joseph to christen the child Jesus, for He would save people from sin. Now study the Sermon on the Mount again and again: is that not a Light that saves you from the darkness of sin? Every word of it exhorts you to turn away from sin and enter the Kingdom of Heaven, the Kingdom of God. By His own glorious life Lord Jesus had kept the doors to the Kingdom of God wide open for people of all times to enter. The Lord's life here was nothing but a living commentary on that Sermon.

Jesus was God Himself. The Holy Scripture reminds us of this fact again and again. Yet, why did He have to endure so much of persecution and suffering? Could He not have by a mere exercise of His Divine Will overwhelmed His foes? Yes. But the Supreme Incarnation of Love that Lord Jesus was, had willed it that His own life would be an example for people to emulate. Therefore, He behaved like any other human being;

and while so doing, fully demonstrated in His own brief but eventful life the Great Sermon that He gave on the Mount.

Both at the very commencement and at the conclusion of the Sermon, He emphatically declares that it is the sacred duty of all those who have had the blessed privilege of hearing the saving Message, *to do and to teach* the commandments, to others. The Lord wants that your light should "shine before men," not for your own glorification, but in order that "they may see your *good works* and glorify your Father which is in Heaven." Practise the Sermon on the Mount. Inspire other children of the Lord by precept as well as by example, to practise the glorious teachings it contains. Thus would the supreme mission of Lord Jesus, the mission of saving people from sin, be fulfilled. It is all the more urgent today that the Message of the Lord should spread throughout the world; for, once again mankind is rushing headlong towards destruction, towards unrighteousness, towards hatred and war. Only the Lord's Message can save the world today. The Divine words of the Sermon on the Mount should be engraved on the tablet of the heart of each man and woman today; and then and then alone can mankind know peace and prosperity.

Cosmic Love

The very first commandment is so thrilling. It is in the Lord's characteristic style of building up a climax. Prior to that day, it was considered unrighteous to kill any being. Killing itself is the grossest manifestation of a feeling that stirs in the heart of man. The Lord wants to save man from this feeling; He suggests therefore a sovereign remedy that would at once cure him of the root cause of the dangerous disease that manifests itself in murder. Anger! Anger is the greatest enemy of man. It destroys intelligence and under its sway man degenerates into something worse than a beast. The Lord exhorts you to get rid of this anger. Even to give verbal vent to this undivine emotion is sin. Do not use abusive words towards anyone; all are children of thy Father. All are your own brothers and sisters. In everyone the Lord dwells. Do not call anyone "a fool." In His divine instruction the Lord goes still further than that. The dire enemy of man should be driven out of his heart. Not only that, in that heart the opposite virtue, love, should be installed. How beautifully He puts it! If this is not done, your worship of God Who is All-Love, is hypocritical. Therefore, when you approach His altar, if an inimical thought arises in you, better leave the altar. Go to the person with whom you have a misunderstanding or quarrel. Get reconciled to him. Become friendly with him once again; and then worship God.

Try this today. This is not an intellectual doctrine to be understood. It is the word of God to be put into practice. Do it now and see for yourself. What a great joy and peace you experience in your worship and in your meditation, if you have washed away all ill-feelings from your heart with the waters of cosmic love!

When your heart is filled with cosmic love, who can be your enemy? Someone else may entertain inimical feelings towards you; but in your heart the feeling of enmity should never arise. To you, he too, is a brother, to be treated with the same love and consideration that you would have for the best of your friends. Jesus would not leave the least room for misunderstanding; ambiguity is foreign to Him. Instruction cannot be more practical than the way He has given it.

"Love your enemies; bless them that curse you; do good to them that hate you, and pray for them which despitefully use you and persecute you." What a convincing argument He brings in support of this holy commandment! Why should you love your enemies? Not because you are greater than they! But because such is the nature of God in whose image you are made, and whose children you—and all—are.

Is the atheist denied God's blessings? The very life-breath which the atheist uses in denying the very existence of God, is provided by Him. "He maketh His Sun to rise on the evil and on the good, and sendeth the rain on the just and on the unjust." Hatred ceaseth not by hatred; hatred ceaseth by love. Love conquers hatred and enmity. Righteousness conquers unrighteousness eventually. Love transforms the heart of man. There is no better way of winning over an enemy, and of transforming an evil-minded person, than to love him and to let him see in your own daily actions the glory of righteous living.

Love and righteousness should become part of your very nature. They should not be feigned nor artificial. Therefore, when Lord Jesus commanded that you should not resist evil, He alluded to His own instruction that love should become your very nature. It requires extraordinary faith in God, realisation of His Omnipotence, understanding the power of love, and supreme moral courage, not to resist evil, but "whosoever shall smite thee on thy right cheek, to turn to him the other also."

By thus not resisting the evil and by demonstrating such love even in the face of evil, you are arousing the latent moral conscience in the evil-minded man. If you had adopted the policy of "an eye for an eye and a tooth for a tooth," the moral conscience in the other person would be completely buried under the evil example you place before him. But, when a man smites you on your cheek and, instead of getting it back "in the same coin," experiences your love, the righteous way you reacted, he is bound to be profoundly influenced by your example; and he would sooner or later reflect over the incident, repent for his action and regain his moral conscience.

The Law Courts in the world could as well be closed down and people enabled to live in peace and amity, if people practise this rule: "If any man will sue you at the law, and take away thy coat, let him have thy cloak also." Does the Lord want you to sit idly and watch yourself being cheated and robbed? No! He wants you to be positively charitable: He wants you to run to the succour of the needy. If he robs you of your coat, because he needs it, better give him your cloak also, so that he would be more comfortable. In reality, along with your cloak, you are giving him the priceless gift of wisdom; he sees in your action the true nature of love, the glory of charity and indifferent attitude of a man-of-God towards the objects of this world. The cloak (the worldly object) is perishable and you are going to part with it one day or the other; but the fruit of the gift, the reward of the charity—especially giving it to the man who would rob you of it—is immortality for you and inner transformation for him. It requires not only moral courage and love, but a supreme dispassion for the object of the world, to practise this. And, Lord Jesus significantly asks: "What availeth man, if he gains the world, but loseth the soul?" The loss of all the objects of the world is nothing compared to the acquisition of this one virtue: charity.

The Practice of Purity

Then comes purity. Here, again, we see how Lord Jesus goes to the very root of the problem and suggests a radical cure. Immorality is not confined to action; it is rooted in the very thought. It can be effectively eliminated not by merely restraining the external organs, as the hypocrites do, but by making the mind and heart pure. "Whosoever looketh on a woman to lust after her hath committed adultery with her already in the heart." Sin is in the mind; the body is a mere tool of the mind.

An extraordinary injunction follows this declaration. It is the method of self-punishment. It is a well-recognised spiritual practice. Punish yourself and pray. Dissociate yourself from the body and even the mind, and chastise them with the rod of self-punishment. First the grosser forms of self-punishment, like fasting, etc., till you learn the technique of completely dissociating yourself from the body and mind and then you can use your strong and powerful will as the reins to restrain the turbulent mind and senses. That is what the Lord alludes to when He says: "And if *thy* right eye offend *thee*, pluck it out, and cast it from thee." You are different from the offending organ; use your discrimination and cut off its supply of soul-force, thought-power and nerve-impulse. Then it will cease to function at variance with your will, but will meekly submit to thy will. This rule applies not only to the eradication of lust, but to anger, too, and the host of other vices. This is panacea for all evils that assail the human heart.

For, remember, that the goal is to be "perfect, even as your Father which is in Heaven is perfect." Perfection in all virtues is what is aimed at; but when you cultivate the cardinal virtues which the Lord has enumerated and dwelt upon in the Sermon on the Mount, the other virtues will cling to you. Love, Purity and Truth; Charity, Humility, Sincerity and Self-surrender—these are great virtues that you should make positive efforts to cultivate. They will make you perfect: a radiant image of God.

Divorce Is Undivine

The ideal of life divine which He places before you is something very grand and leaves no loopholes at all. He wants that you should not only shun evil but that you should not cause another person to fall into evil. Modern civilisation has conclusively proved that the practice of divorce demoralises man and woman, wrecks the happiness of domestic life, ruins the very life of the children; and, when peace at home is lost, it is lost in man's heart, too—and this disharmony spreads to other fields of human activity. Therefore, Lord Jesus calls him an adulterer who puts away his wife. Divorce is undivine! and the sooner it is abandoned, the better for mankind.

Self-Surrender: Key to Truth

In the practice of Truth, the Lord has something very illuminating to say. People generally swear that what they say is the truth; and they swear that they would do certain things in the future. Lord Jesus asks His followers to abstain from swearing. Swearing springs from the self-arrogating ego. It is vanity. No one really knows the truth: but everyone is ready to swear "by God" that what he says is the truth. It is arrogant vehemence. A wise man would say: "To the best of my knowledge and belief, this is the truth." Only God knows what is truth. And, therefore, Lord Jesus says: *"Judge not others."*

The other form of swearing is to swear for the future. One can take resolves with a devout prayer. This is more like auto-suggestion. You may say: "Henceforth, I shall lead a life of abstinence, of celibacy or of renunciation; God, shower Thy Grace on me." This is necessary for spiritual progress. Similarly in the case of worldly dealings. It is necessary to enter into some agreements and undertakings. But the most important point to bear in mind always—and this is the fundamental tenet of true religious life—is that the future is in His Hands. Our outlook upon the future ought to be one of surrender to the Divine Will. To pledge ourselves to certain vows is like a little boy promising his fond mother that he would "for ever and ever wear the beautiful coat" she presented him on his fifth birthday.

It is here that the greatest caution is needed. One should neither surrender to the evil forces of nature (Satan), nor should one develop religious arrogance. To lead an aimless life, taking things as they come along, reacting instinctively to surroundings and circumstances is subhuman. To arrogate to oneself the powers of doing or undoing things, of shaping his own and mankind's destinies, is surely more than an animal can do; but it is something *worse*—it is diabolical. The wise man, on the other hand, would look forward to something good, will aspire for something grand, will work for peace and prosperity, and then *leave everything to His Will*. He knows that by his own will, he cannot "make one hair white or black" on his own head!

This is the master-key to all progress. For thus recognising the inevitability of the Divine Will, man will march forward, with God enthroned forever in his heart, assimilating all that is good everywhere and during changing times, and transforming all that is base and evil, by the touch of his godliness, forbearance and love. He will not be bound down by dogmas and "fixed" creeds and rituals, but he will be lifted up on the wings of God's Will and His Grace.

Shun Insincerity

Humility and prayer are the channels through which His Grace flows towards the seeker and Grace directs him towards the fulfilment of His Will. It is in Grace that the individual will finds oneness with the Divine Will; and Grace is obtained through real humility and constant prayer.

Therefore, Lord Jesus warns us from making a show of our religious life. Incidentally, He reveals a very great secret. Sincerity is an all-important factor in not only spiritual life, but in the daily life of every human being. Insincerity is falsehood, to be shunned with greater vigilance than that with which one would discard a poisonous "fruit." The poison in the tempting form of a fruit is ruinous to the physical body; insincerity in the holy garb of a righteous life is ruinous to the very soul of man. An act of charity done publicly for the acclamation of society might earn a good reward here, in name and fame, in social status and material comforts. But it has very little spiritual value. For, God the Indweller looks to the innermost motives. He knows that the motive is not to earn His Grace or to do His Will, but to acquire the goods of this world. And, this is the very antithesis of the life divine.

He who would lead the divine life, therefore, would do charity, not because it would earn him name and fame, but because charity is the reflection of the God-in-man. None of His Supreme Blessings—the sun, the rain, the wind and the life-sustaining earth—beats its drums and proclaims, "It is I who maintain your life and enable you to live and function here." God, hidden in all these great channels of His Grace and instruments of His Will, showers His Blessings on us. The seeker who seeks to do His Will, will likewise consider himself an instrument of His Will and a channel of His Grace and that, therefore, it is natural for him to be charitable and loving. Charity and universal love become part of his very nature, and not something extraordinary to be bragged about.

God, the Indweller, is well pleased with such a seeker and rewards him "openly". The seeker becomes a saint, a man-of-God, radiating divinity. People are charmed in his very presence and adore and worship him.

Similarly in the case of prayer and fasting. These are natural to a real seeker. Prayer is his spiritual food; and fasting is a natural corollary to it. He denies material food to his mind and senses so that he can, through prayer, feed them with spiritual manna. And this is the process of divinising oneself thoroughly. It is done, not to win the favour of any human being, but in order that one's own inner personality may be divinised. What, then, is the meaning of making a show of prayer and fasting?

Lord's Prayer

If God's Will is done here and His Grace alone fills and surrounds us on all sides, what are we to pray for? Lord Jesus reminds you: "your Father knoweth what things ye have need of, before ye ask Him." The prayer is, therefore for His Grace, for constantly remembering Him, for making you a channel to do His Will, and for forgiveness. There is a mysterious power in the universe—Satan—that tempts even the best of men, deludes even the wisest of them, and leads even the greatest of them astray. Prayer is offered to the Lord to guard you against this. Therefore, Lord Jesus has framed a beautiful prayer:

> Our Father which art in heaven,
> Hallowed be Thy name.
> Thy kingdom come,
> Thy will be done,
> On earth as it is in heaven.
>
> Give us this day our daily bread;
> And forgive us our debts,
> As we forgive our debtors;
> And lead us not into temptation,
> But deliver us from evil.
>
> For Thine is the kingdom,
> The power and the Glory,
> For ever and ever, Amen.

The "daily bread" is not merely the physical bread or the food that we give the body to keep it alive. For, the Lord assures you that God knows your need and, even as He clothes the lilies in the field with rich and delightful colour and feeds the fowls of the air, He will feed you and clothe you without your praying for them. Meditate upon this and realise God's Supreme Grace that gave you and that sustains your life. You will clearly understand the meaning of His Immortal utterance: "Lay not up for yourselves treasures upon earth, where moth and rust doth corrupt, and where thieves break through and steal; but lay up for yourselves treasures in Heaven, where neither moth nor rust doth corrupt, and where thieves do not break through nor steal." By thus revolutionising the values alone can dispassion arise in the heart and the Kingdom of God realised in one's own heart. "For where your treasure is, there will your heart be also." Develop discrimination. Care not for the riches of this world; they are perishable and they cannot give you lasting peace and happiness. Devote yourself to the acquisition of spiritual wealth by regular prayer, meditation and charity. This prayer to the Lord is, therefore, for spiritual bread, spiritual food,—in other words, for devotion to Him and for right discrimination. "Seek ye first the Kingdom of God, and His righteousness; and all these things shall be added unto you," said He.

Give Up Fault-finding

Having said all this, Lord Jesus proceeds to utter a stern warning to His followers against a very common, but highly disastrous human failing: that of finding fault in others. This again is the work of the ego in man. It seeks to cover up its own deficiencies by discovering faults in others. Man is generally so greatly concerned about others' weaknesses and sins,—not that he wants to correct them, but to establish his superiority over them!—that he hardly ever bestows a thought on the million defects that gnaw at his vitals. Who would like to feel that there are formidable deficiencies in one's own inner makeup? Only a spiritual hero would resolutely turn one's gaze within and introspect, carrying on a searching self-analysis and strive to perfect himself. Lord Jesus wants everyone of you to be a spiritual hero, not a vain scandal-monger. *"Why beholdest thou the mote that is in thy brother's eye, but considerest not the beam that is in thy own eye?"* He asks, *"Thou hypocrite, first cast out the beam out of thine own eye; and then shalt thou see clearly to cast out the mote out of thy brother's eye."* This is very, very serious warning that every seeker after Truth would do well to bear always in mind.

The Golden Rule

The Sermon concludes with the same glowing words of wisdom that is characteristic of every word that Lord Jesus uttered during the course of His spiritual ministry. He does not encourage indiscriminate preaching; the seeker after Truth must be initiated into Its mysteries. He who hungers after wisdom must be fed with the spiritual food of divine knowledge. *"For everyone that asketh receiveth. . . Or what man is there of you, whom if his son asketh bread, will he give him a stone?"* The Gracious Lord listens to everyone's prayer and fulfils everyone's pious and noble aspirations. Even so, His Chosen Messengers ought to give the Truth to the seeker in a way that would be suited to the stage of evolution and temperament of the seeker.

The righteous way of life should be pointed out to all; whatever men seek they should be helped to attain by righteous means. It is unwise to preach high philosophy to a man who is starving and is unable to keep body and soul together! You should help him find the way to earn his bread through righteous means. In time he would discover the life divine.

Here Lord Jesus gives the Golden Rule of Right Conduct. What is the fundamental principle of righteousness? *"All things whatsoever ye would that men should do to you, do ye even so to them; for this is the law."* This is the supreme law of righteous conduct.

The Life Divine

How simple, glorious and grand is the life divine! Yet, "few there be that find it," says Lord Jesus. What we see around us today amply justifies this prophetic utterance of the Saviour: *"Because strait is the gate and narrow is the way which leadeth unto life."* The objects of the world which promise immediate sense-satisfaction and physical comfort are so tempting that man instinctively grabs at them. But they lead him to destruction—to the destruction of the one great gift of the Lord that serves as the light of his life, viz., discrimination. It is discrimination that distinguishes man from animal. But by leading a sensual life he has degenerated into an animal. "If the light that is in thee be darkness, how great is that darkness!" How true! If the power of discrimination that the Lord has bestowed upon man be made to subserve the animal instincts of man, the craving for sense pleasures, what wonder is there that he degenerates into something worse than even an animal? Lord Jesus warns: "No man can serve two masters: ye cannot serve God and Mammon." Mammon promises immediate physical pleasure which lures man away, along the broadway towards destruction. "Ye are the salt of the earth but if the salt have lost his savour, wherewith shall it be salted?" If man, the crown of God's creation, has lost his power of discrimination; if he, made in the image of God, chooses the path of evil, what will happen to civilisation, to humanity? He will lead the whole world to destruction.

The very intelligence which God has been gracious enough to give him, he will use to support his destructive actions. How many leaders we see in the various spheres of human life, who are but misleaders of mankind! "Beware of false prophets which come to you in sheep's clothing, but inwardly they are ravening wolves."

How shall we know them? "Ye shall know them by their fruits. Do men gather grapes of thorns or figs of thistles?" What a thrilling message! What inspiring words of wisdom! What a clear guidance! Watch their actions. Are they in accordance with the Commandments of Lord Jesus? Do they conform to the Holiest Message of Lord—the Sermon on the Mount? If not, reject them.

You have the Lord's Living Presence in the Words of the Sermon on the Mount. They are not Words. They are the very life-breath of the Eternal and Immortal Lord Jesus. They are simple, direct, divine and soul-stirring instructions directed by a Divine Being to the very core of your heart. Enshrine this Sermon on the tablet of your heart. Lord Jesus from within you, will guide you along the glorious path of Eternal Life to the Kingdom of God where you will forever enjoy perennial peace and eternal bliss. May the choicest blessings of Lord Jesus be on you all!

Chapter Four

CHRISTMAS MESSAGES
of
SRI SWAMI SIVANANDA

1945

DIVINISE THY NATURE!

All memorable occasions, all holy days and sacred anniversaries carry a message and a higher call to those who will hear and respond. They invariably form a reminder of the true mission and central purpose of human life. The Call of Christmas is the Call to a new Birth in the Spirit. Its message is the lofty one of the Divine Life, the Christ-Life of Compassion, Truth and Purity. That moment is the real joyous Christmas to you when the Divine Consciousness that shone through Jesus blossoms and lights up the inner chambers of thy heart. Christmas to you is that day you start to lead the divine life of Satya (truth), Ahimsa (non-violence) and Brahmacharya (chastity) that the great Vedanti of the West lived. Many a Christmas has come and gone. Celebrations are held every year but have you risen in answer to its Divine Call? Has the Divine Child taken birth in the inner Bethlehem of your heart? It is the wanton neglect of man to hear this call and divinise his life that has brought upon humanity the horrors of war, disease, sufferings and restlessness.

Two thousand years ago Divinity incarnated upon this planet to show to all Humanity the glorious path to everlasting Life by actually living the Divine Life upon this earth. The great Jesus embodied in Himself the triple quality of Satya, Ahimsa and absolute Brahmacharya. During the entire duration of His sublime life, Christ lived as the visible expression of the highest Truth. He was a living witness to the Supreme Reality essentially indwelling in Man. In His dealing with the outside world, He was verily Ahimsa incarnate. With words brimming with the true spirit of Ahimsa He preaches the doctrine of non-retaliation. "Present thy left cheek to the assailant that smites thee on the right. If a man takes away thy coat forcibly, offer him thy cloak too."

No test, struggle, torment or persecution whatsoever could ruffle Him up to wrath or retaliation. In His personal life He was indeed Purity Itself. Unless ye become like little children you cannot enter the Kingdom of Heaven. You have to be absolutely pure like the innocent little ones. One of the greatest examples of Naishthika Brahmacharya, strict celibacy and spotless chastity Mankind has in Jesus, the Christ. He mentions how some men "make eunuchs of themselves" for the sake of the Kingdom of Heaven. Thus the threefold strand of Ahimsa, Satya and Brahmacharya were woven into the very fabric of the Divine Life that Jesus lived.

An almost supernal spotless purity rested like a divine mantle upon His sublime personality. His life was a wonderful combination of Jnana, Bhakti and Karma, based upon a supreme Para Vairagya. An ideal integral development of head, heart and hand has rendered His life a model for mankind to emulate for all eternity. Christ was ever conscious of His inseparable identity with the Supreme Self. Yet deep devotion and love for the personal God constantly found expression in Him in the form of prayers, praises and glorification. And in His actual day-to-day life He was the very personification of the spirit of Karma Yoga. His entire life was a continuous ministry unto the afflicted. His feet moved but to reach where aid was needed. If His hands moved it was but to help the troubled and oppressed. His tongue spoke only to utter soft, honeyed words of compassion, consolation, inspiration and enlightenment. With the very glances of His luminous Yogic eyes Jesus awakened, elevated and transformed those whom he gazed upon. He felt, thought, talked and acted for the good of others. Amidst this all He dwelt in the unbroken awareness of the assertion "I and my Father are one." His life was that of a Sage in Sahaja Samadhi.

In Jesus the Man, the aspirant or the Sadhaka finds two traits to be faithfully emulated, namely, an admirable moral courage in being witness to Truth. His life displays a silent yet supreme heroism in the face of the most determined opposition, persecution and misunderstanding. And He has set an example how a true seeker repulses the temptations on the spiritual path. Long before the outward drama of crucifixion, Jesus voluntarily crucified Himself spiritually by annihilating the lower self and living a purely divine life.

The great Rishi that He was, the Man of Galilee exemplified in Himself the "Sthitadheeh Muni" Lord Krishna describes in the sacred Gita. Jesus was for ever the Self-absorbed Sage, perfectly balanced in the midst of opposites. He never lost His calm even for a single moment of His intensely-lived life. He neither rejoiced in pleasure nor grieved in pain. Looking with perfect equal vision upon friend and foe, intent only upon universal weal, this perfected Siddha Purusha typifies that magnanimous state of *"Sarva dharman parityajya mamekam saranam vraja,"* the compassionate voice of this God-Man called aloud to all mankind "Come unto me, all ye that are weary and heavy-laden" and promised to "relieve their burden" and grant them rest. Come! Come! Come! was the divine call. And how? Casting thy care upon Him for He careth for thee. Thy work is to intently think of Him and Him alone. Never care for anything else for does He not look after the "lilies in the field and the birds in the air?" Depend on Him and He will care for thee for *"Ananyaschintayanto mam ye janah paryupasate; Tesham nityabhiyuktanam yogakshemam vahamyaham"* is the promise of Lord Krishna.

You know how at Jesus's birth a bright guiding Star appeared in the in the sky to lead the Magii to the Divine Child. Take this as Your Christmas Star. May this show you the way to lead the Life Divine as exemplified in the mystic and Yogi of Bethlehem! Manifest the same Living Reality, the Spotless Purity and the lofty Divine compassion. Divinise thy life. Lead the Divine Life.

1949

CHRISTMAS MESSAGE

Beloved Children of the Christ!

The Holy Christmas approaches us all once again. On this sacred occasion, I send you my warmest greetings and my best wishes for the birth of Lord Jesus in your heart!

It is good to rejoice; it is good to feel and to radiate joy and happiness, especially on an occasion which marks the Coming of One Who pointed out to us the Way to Bliss. But, you who have taken up the Holy Yoga and who tread the Path of Divine Life, have a special responsibility. It is to meditate on Lord Jesus, recollect His Teachings and propagate by practice and precept His Life-giving Message.

Christ, Krishna, Buddha and Mohammed all lead us to the same gate that opens out into a Heaven of LOVE—a love that does not admit of hatred, even as the light in the sun knows no darkness. May Lord Jesus reveal Himself to you! May you become an embodiment of His Teachings! May you shine as a True Christian, a true and faithful descendant of the Lord! May the blessings of Lord Jesus be upon you!

1951

CHRIST: THE PRINCE OF PEACE

Adorations and obeisance to Jesus, the Christ, the Divine Messenger of love, goodwill and peace!

Blessed indeed is mankind that it still cherishes and honours devotedly the hallowed memory of this great Light that descended upon and illumined our earth nearly two thousand years ago. So long as the people keep alive in their hearts the great ideal of Divine Life as lived by Jesus, and so long as they heed His message of goodness, humility, purity, harmlessness and true, motiveless love for all beings, till then are assured unto them happiness, prosperity, welfare, security, peace and goodwill.

A firm living faith as well as a willing adherence to Christ's Gospel of Love and Compassion do indeed form the only real basis of happiness here and hereafter, and of abiding peace to mankind. The Christ-life of humility, silent endurance, utter simplicity, purity, all embracing love and deep prayerfulness are the unfailing guarantee for the resurrection of man from his present state of "civilised" barbarity into which he has plunged headlong during the recent years.

O Man! Fried as thou art in the flames of hatred, fear, greed, jealousy, anger, enmity and mutual destruction, perishing in the fierce furnace of deluded, materialistic life, turn away now and resolve to abandon, on this sacred occasion, all these satanic elements. Heal and cool thyself in the stream of Divine Life that flows from the sacred feet of the Fountain Divine, Lord Jesus. Fill thyself with the Light of Divine Joy. Be refreshed in the living waters of the Christ Consciousness.

Christ is the Prince of Peace. All things conducive to the creation of Peace, individual as well as universal, comprise indeed the true allegiance to this Divine King of kings. Any thought, act, word or course of conduct that disturbs the state of peace, verily implies the denial of the Lord's Grace Incarnate, a disowning of our link with this embodiment of Divinity.

On this sacred occasion of Christmas, let all awaken within their bosom a consciousness of the Christ Ideal and determine to live henceforth the true Divine Life as preached by Jesus in His famous Sermon on the Mount. In that unforgettable divine message, the Great Jesus has given to you all the pattern for the ideal life upon earth, a pattern which if followed will, without fail, lift you from the gross life to a transcendental Divine Life in the Spirit. You find here the highest Vedanta presented in the simplest of words, "Love thy neighbour as thyself."

The teaching of Jesus is applicable to followers of all Faiths. His was not a pharisaical doctrine. His doctrine of the Kingdom of Heaven was a call for a complete change and utter cleansing of the earthly life. Christianity can flourish only in the spirit of give and take. A Christian should be as humble and as tolerant as Jesus. Only then would he appeal to the followers of other religions.

May the blessings of Lord Jesus be upon you all!

1953

STRAIN OF AN ETERNAL GOSPEL

On the 25th of this month we will be celebrating the advent of the Blessed Messiah, the nineteen hundred and sixty-first birth Anniversary of Jesus, for it is generally accepted that He saw the light of the day in the eighth year before the Christian calendar began. Incidentally, modern historians and paleographic experts are inclined to believe that Jesus was born sometime in the month of October rather than in the night of December 25, but reason we have none to wrangle over this dispute, because it is hardly that traditional beliefs change and our concern is only with the life and teachings of the Christ.

How can mortal thought and finite language describe the glory of such a one who was far above the flesh with so profound, fathomless, immutable and yet so humane, loving and compassionate a personality that it is difficult even to imagine that once he had actually breathed this air and trodden over this earth?

A Revolutionary Doctrine

The doctrine of Jesus was surely one of the most powerful revolutionary forces to galvanise human thought. He lived far ahead of his time, so that the world of the day utterly failed to appreciate the real significance of His teaching and considered

Him to be a dangerous blasphemer. No wonder then that the Jewish Pharisees found their only redress in arresting and prosecuting this noble, relentless and redoubtable crusader at the Jerusalem court of Pilate, the Roman magistrate, who finally decided to get rid of Him by a barbarously slow execution upon the cross, so that a religious uprising with consequent political complications might be nipped in the bud.

One of the earliest and most enlightened prophets of spiritual socialism, baptised by John while He was about thirty and preaching in the Aramaic tongue in Judea during the reign of Tiberius Caesar, Jesus Christ was first to advocate in that part of the world the necessity to shed racial and class bigotry and to identify oneself as a common member of the vast family of mankind where everyone was a child of God with equal rights and opportunities to live in peace and to seek Him.

When selfishness and greed were nothing to be ashamed of, it was Jesus who emphasised the necessity of equal distribution of wealth, practical sympathy and loving considerateness for the fellowmen and the strangers alike, of abandoning vengeance and reprisal through forgiveness and charity, to love one's neighbour as one's own self for the obvious reason that there might be no disunity and disharmony, and, on the whole, to encounter evil by good, because if evil was to be met by evil there would be no end of it.

Christ's Concept of God

In the Hebrew world, Jesus was first to bring a healthier and more rational concept of God. The Jews believed that God had agreed to a bargain with Father Abraham, deciding their fate arbitrarily and yet reserving special privileges for them over other tribesmen in His own kingdom. This idea was revolting to Christ, and He boldly spoke out that God had nothing to do with one man's comfort and another's suffering, that He was a loving Father to all mankind, claiming no favourites absolutely: impartial, kind and merciful, and knowable through the cleansing of the human nature.

In Palestine, when Jesus lived, tribal loyalties and distinctions were rigidly observed, and, as is the case even in our own time, one race looked upon another with contempt and despise and tried to glorify themselves above all. Jesus could not bear this and sought to break up all differentiation through the gospel of universal brotherhood and all-inclusive love. This was one of the reasons, together with his unchangeable conviction in the common fatherhood of God, that outraged the sectarian patriotic fervour of his own people and the preferential, divine hierarchy of the priestcraft. He could neither reconcile Himself that there were to be accumulated private property, reserved considerations, justification for earthly pride or for indiscriminate satiation of base impulses, continuation of traditional habits which sought to set up barriers between men and atonement for one's misdeeds through monetary dividends. What was the result? Jesus had to be a martyr.

His Religion

His religion of the Messiah was the religion of heart, built on the edifice of love. He said that the Kingdom of God was not to be found in this material world of fraud and deceit but in the hearts of good people who had transformed their lower nature. Thus, first of all, Jesus advocated an inner purification and He applied this doctrine on a social basis through His commandments in which He asked not to be promiscuous, not to steal, not to kill, not to bear false witness, not to hate and cavil, and not to defraud. But He went further and said if one really wanted to enter the Kingdom of God, he had to renounce earthly riches and vanities. So strong was His reaction to the privileged wealthy class, knowing fully well how corrupting was the influence of gold, that He proclaimed, 'It is easier for a camel to enter the eye of a needle than for the rich man to enter into the Kingdom of God,' and to a seeker who wanted to inherit the eternal life, He said, 'Ye cannot serve God and Mammon; for either ye will hate one and love the other, or else ye will hold to the one and despise the other. Renounce everything, take the cross and follow me.'

His Teaching

Christ had an immense conviction about the sacredness of what He taught, emphatic as he was in His Sermon on the Mount that 'Blessed are they that hungered and thirsted after righteousness, for they shall be filled; blessed are the merciful, for they shall obtain mercy; blessed are the pure in heart, for they shall see God; and blessed are the peace-makers, for they shall be called the sons of God.'

He believed in the law of Cause and Effect, for He remarked 'Whatever man soweth that shall he also reap.' Many have wrongly accused Him of being unduly exuberant in His promises for a future blessedness in heaven. On the contrary, He concerned Himself more with the present than with the distant future, since he asked people to live the day well in goodness and in the service of God, and 'take no thought for the morrow, for the morrow shall take thought for the things of itself.'

Jesus revealed a profound respect for the public sentiment when He said 'the voice of the people is the voice of God.' He had an utter repugnance for religious insincerity, for He was very particular in advising 'When thou prayeth thou shalt not be as the hypocrites are, for they love to pray standing in the synagogues and in the corners of the streets that may be seen of men; but thou, when prayeth, enter into thy closet, and when thou hast shut thy door, pray to thy Father which is in secret, and thy Father which seeth in secret shall reward thee openly.'

If Jesus Appears Today

It is extremely doubtful if by chance Christ happened to appear in this world again whether people would really listen to Him even at this time, in spite of the tremendous proselytising by the unending trails of zealous missionaries, and, after all, whether the West itself, the very home of Christianity, would be willing to change its ways from so tantalising a glamour of materialism and its myriads of vested commercial and industrial interests, no doubt all meant for the greater and wider comforts of the fellowmen, but nonetheless resulting in an unsatiable whetting of epicurean tendencies and the headiness of power politics. At any rate, Jesus might most likely find himself a stranger if He happened to be in the aisle of a Synod. Besides, nearly half of Europe and two thirds of Asia will decidedly refuse Him entry visa, and more than eight hundred millions of people will be debarred from access to Him. And yet, the world has no other go but to listen to and practise the teaching of the Christ if it is to save itself from recurrent global conflagrations, inevitable slaughter of great masses of innocent people, unmitigable suffering, and systematic demoralisation.

The pealing of Christmas bells brings us a wistful rag of hope and a languid expectation that the spirit of the Messiah might one day resurrect in all its glory in the hearts of men and women all over the world, and particularly within those that are at the helms of the world and governments.

May the grace of Holy Christ be upon us all!

1954

I

THE CHRIST-LIFE MUST BE LIVED

Jesus Christ lived and symbolised divine consciousness. He was the very personification of divinity. He was born at a time when ignorance, superstition, greed, hatred and hypocrisy prevailed upon India, as elsewhere. The rulers were arrogant and unrighteous. The people were avaricious, indolent and heedless. Purity was forgotten. Morality was neglected. They were more intent upon worshiping Mammon than adoring God. There was no idealism.

In the midst of these conditions, Christ was born and he worked a transformation in the lives of the people, though not quite successfully in His life time but through the following centuries by the means of His teachings. He gave a new spiritual turn to the lives of His fellowmen. Thus a new era dawned upon this world, and the teaching of Jesus spread far and wide.

Before discrimination and spiritual awakening dawn within the seeker, he has bigoted outlook, selfish tendencies and no thought for God or the higher divine life. He is then immersed in the pursuit of material interests. He is a slave of his senses. He has no spiritual ideal in life. He is desire ridden. Arrogance, avarice and sensuality characterise his personality. He lives a life of lust, anger, greed, deluded attachment, pride, egoism and jealousy.

If this state of things must cease and the seeker must enter into a new life of spiritual aspiration, purity and devotion, then the Christ spirit must take its birth within one's heart. That will be the real adoration of Jesus Christ. That will be the true following of Christianity. When the divine element that is dormant within us begins to express itself, then indeed we open ourselves to the grace of the Christ. From then onward light begins to shine where darkness was before. Ignorance gives place to the beginning of wisdom. Impurity is replaced by purity. Hatred ceases and love begins to blossom forth.

In his innermost core, man is essentially divine. But through the medium of the human personality two forces keep acting. They are the forces of good and evil, light and darkness. The divine and the undivine both operate in the human consciousness. To completely overcome and eradicate the undivine elements and to fully manifest the supreme divine Consciousness in all its radiant light and glory is to be achieved through the living of the Christ-life in the utmost faithful detail. That is spiritual life. That is Yoga. That is Sadhana. That is the path of Self-realisation.

If the Christ-life is to be lived, first of all the child Christ has to be born in our heart. Only then does the real spiritual life commence for the aspirant. The first manifestation of the divine urge to progress in the path of goodness and virtue and to cherish noble ideals and eradicate vicious, negative tendencies signifies the birth of the infant Jesus in our consciousness. From hence starts the living of the Christ-life in all its details of sublime purity, faith in divinity, mercy, compassion, love, selflessness, desirelessness, egolessness, forgiveness, prayerfulness and so on. Hence starts the life of earnest Yoga, of self-restraint and simplicity, of unbroken serenity and peace, tolerance, balance of mind in pleasure and pain, unflinching courage and determination, and perfect dedication to the worship of God through the service of humanity. This is the spiritual implication of all the celebrations connected with Jesus Christ. This is also the message of the Easter.

With the advent of this Christ-spirit within the heart of a truly earnest seeker, all mundane desires come to an end. There is a cessation of all vicious tendencies in him. He begins to influence others around him. The spirit of Jesus Christ emanates from him. Many are made aware of that spirit and a great deal of good is brought into their lives. Thus, if every individual begins to live a new life of divine aspiration, fellow-feeling and social service, spirituality will gradually overcome materialism. There will be more of goodwill, more of harmony and more of peace in this world. The tendency to help each other, to understand each other and to decrease avariciousness, selfishness and egoism will grow gradually in every sphere, which would mean greater happiness in every hearth and home.

Spiritual life is neither exclusively meant for the poor and the lowly, nor is it beyond the reach of the wealthy. To pursue the spiritual path one need not seek the undisturbed assurity of food and shelter. But there is a significant point in the birth of Jesus. He was born in a simple, lowly place, a corner of a stable. Also he was born in darkness, in the obscure hour of midnight, when no one even knew about it, except a few blessed souls. The significance here is that spiritual awakening comes to the seeker who is humble and meek and simple. The light of divine consciousness dawns only when the delusive glitters of material glamour and the corruptive influence of wealth are absent.

The quality of true humility is one of the indispensable fundamentals. Only when there are simplicity, holiness and renunciation of all earthly desires and the pride of learning, goodness and merit, the divine light manifests within. Even as Christ was born unknown to the world and in the obscurity of darkness, so also the advent of the Christ spirit takes place in the inwardness of the soul when there is total self-effacement and self abnegation. Where the urge of aggrandisement and vanity abides, there divinity cannot unfold itself, for these expressions of egotism are permanent hindrances to any kind of spiritual growth. You can be sure, a man of vanity is far from God. A man of selfishness knows nothing of God. A man of intolerance has thoroughly misunderstood God. 'Empty thyself and I shall fill thee,' is the advice of Jesus. The Kingdom of Heaven is surely for the humble in spirit.

It was this secret that centuries ago Jesus explained to Nicodemus. The good man did not quite understand what precisely Jesus meant. 'How can it be? How can I be born again if I am to attain the Kingdom of God?' Asked Nicodemus. Then Christ explained that this birth was an inward transformation, not of the body, but of the spirit. Such inner spiritual birth is essential if one truly wishes to know Jesus Christ.

May the true implication of the Christ-life dawn within every heart! Realise fully that so long as thirst of power and arrogance of wealth infect the nature of man, until then the spirit of Christ is out of reach. As with the individual, even so with the community and the nation. It is only when real spiritual transformation occurs in the hearts of the individuals that its effects can be felt in the nations of the world. Let every soul understand the duty of the human life. Let everyone cultivate a sense of brotherhood, tolerance, charity, humility, mutual understanding, love and compassion. Let everyone aspire for greater knowledge, greater enlightenment and greater goodwill. Let the sense of evolution and perfection be eternally progressive.

II

WHERE ARE YOU, O SAVIOUR?

Jesus! Light of the world! My Saviour! Where are You?

For, in this dark hour when mankind rushes headlong towards its own destruction, there is urgent need for Thee!

Where are You, O Saviour? Have You not promised that You will never leave us comfortless and that You will come to us? This, indeed, is the time when You should reveal Yourself to us so that we might follow You in peace and joy.

Alas, my Good Shepherd! Many of Thy sheep are lost. But, we don't despair. How kind and gracious You are! You take a supreme delight in bringing the lost sheep back to the fold. Each lost sheep adds to Your delight. Come, come, there is great work and greater delight awaiting You.

Where are You, O Saviour? Temples have been built for You all over the world. Literally, there is no part of the globe where people do not profess to be Your followers. Truly, my Lord, the sun never sets over Thy Kingdom on Earth. But, alas, the very people who owe allegiance to You have surrendered themselves to the evil hands of Satan. They seek to serve You on Sundays and Mammon on the rest of the days.

Lord, if a man loves You he will keep Your words, and, the Father will love him and You will come unto him and make Your abode with him. Today people remember Your name but have forgotten Your words—the comforting balm, the invaluable treasure, the fountain of bliss, the nectar of immortality, the philosopher's stone, that transformed man into divinity.

You had given us Your great Commandment: "Love one another, as I have loved you," and You have shown us by Your own life that You could (and did) give up Your life itself for our sake. Not only is such love vanishing from the face of the earth today, but in his greed, fear and hatred, man is ready to cut the throat of his brother. Where are You, O Saviour? Come, come: ere it is too late.

When will people realise that "a man's life consisteth not in the abundance of the things which he possesseth?" When will they seek the Kingdom of God and let the other things be added unto them at His Will? Can there be a warning, stronger and clearer, than Your words: "Take heed and beware of covetousness."

Where are You, O Saviour? Come, come, and remind man that he has in his hands a stone with which he can get two fruits at one stroke. If only he understands aright, and practises Your precept: "Sell that ye have, and give alms, and provide yourselves bags which were to hold a treasure in the heaven that faileth not, where no thief approacheth, neither moth corrupteth," he will not only achieve his own salvation, but will create harmony and peace around him and there will be brotherhood and prosperity in the world.

Where are you, O Saviour? Your children for whom you gave up Your life itself—the poor, the downtrodden, the faithful, the persecuted—are oppressed and are deprived of even the little they have. Their oppressors whom You sought to save through Your life-transforming Message of Love and Oneness, are once again straying away into the path of inequity. You have commended: "When thou makest a feast, call the poor, the maimed, the lame, the blind, and thou shalt be blessed." But, everywhere we see feasts and festivities, dinners and garden parties to which only the friends and rich neighbours are invited! And, what do they do? In Your sage counsels were the seeds of peace and prosperity. Discarding them, they gather only to plot against each other, and together against a third. Come, O Saviour; now is the time for Your clarion call.

Lord! Forget not Your Promise: "Whatever ye shall ask in my name, that will I do." In Your Holy Divine Name, I pray: Come, O Supreme Monarch of the world! Enthrone Yourself in the hearts of all men. Even as You said: without You nothing can be done.

Where are You, O Saviour! "Thou art where Thy Word is." This have You revealed in Your luminous utterances: that You are one with Your Law. This Law is the Law of Unity, of Brotherhood, of Love, of Humility, of Forgiveness, of Righteousness, of Charity. I pray to You, on this Most Holy Day of Your Birth here: take Your birth once again in the hearts of all men and women all over the world and take Your birth in the form of this Divine Law. Thus would humanity be saved, and thus would Jesus, my Lord, the Son of God, be proclaimed as the Eternal Saviour.

Come, Prince of Peace! For Your Second Coming are Your chosen children, the saints and men-of-God all over the world, praying and waiting. Come in the form of Your fiery words. Come in the form of the Sermon on the Mount, every word aglow with Your Divine Light. Coming into man's heart, let Your Word become the blood of his blood, breath of his life, soul of his soul. Only thus transformed into the very images of Your Word shall men regain the Eternal Life, Infinite Joy and Perennial Peace that passeth understanding.

On this Holy Christmas Night, may the Lord be reborn in the hearts of every man and woman in the whole world!

1955

AWAKEN JESUS IN YOU AND FOLLOW HIM

Crores of prostrations to the Lord Jesus, the Beloved Son of God, the Supreme King of kings, the Divine Ruler of the hearts of mankind.

Lord Jesus came into this earth to re-establish the Kingdom of God within the heart of man. Deliverance from sin, from ignorance and delusion, from misery and disease, He brought within your easy reach—if only you grasped it.

Faith is the hand that can grasp it, grasp His Radiant Feet—and what are His Feet but Love and Forgiveness.

Faith, faith is what mankind lacks woefully today. Worse still, mankind has lost faith in the divine realities, and unfortunately pins its faith on the unreal shadow that looms large over its head. Man believes the unreal to be real and doubts the real! That is the work of Maya, Satan.

The simple fishermen of Galilee have set a shining example before us. What did they do when their faith was shaken and the ship was tossed about by the storm? They awakened Jesus and He prayed to the Lord for help.

Surely that is what we must do on this Christmas Day, when the ship of humanity is tossed about by the storm of evil. Take refuge in Lord Jesus. Awaken Him within you. Awaken the Christ-consciousness within you. Yes, He will say: "O ye of little faith, were you afraid?" He will stop the surging waves of destruction, and command the storm of evil to cease. And your faith in Him will be restored, too.

Restore to the soul, faith in its oneness with God—"I and my Father are one," said the Lord. This realisation is the key to perennial peace and eternal bliss.

Restore to the mind faith in the glory of righteousness. Sin is manufactured in the mind; the external organs are only the channels of distribution for this sin. Lord Jesus again and again called upon man to be clean inside. Light the lamp of righteousness in your mind; then you will radiate goodness in all your actions. Be good first; then you will do good.

Restore to the heart faith in the Lord's Love and Mercy. How merciful and loving is the Lord that He renounces His Divine Abode and takes birth here amongst mortals, in this physical place of pain and suffering, in order to bring comfort and solace to man! "Be ye perfect even as the Father in Heaven is Perfect." Let this love and this Mercy guide your actions. Open your heart, with faith in Lord Jesus, so that He might cast out the devil from your heart—the devil of selfishness, the devil of egoism, the devil of lust, anger and greed.

O Man! Wake up now. There stands the Lord in all His divine Majesty and says: "Follow Me." Take up the cross and follow Him. Be ready to sacrifice everything in order to do His Word. Thus would you earn the Kingdom of Heaven. Thus would you reap the richest harvest of Immortality and Eternal Bliss; and the world inhabited by such followers of Lord Jesus will be the Abode of Peace, Plenty and Prosperity.

May the choicest blessings of the Saviour be upon you all, this joyous Christmas!

1956

PRAYER IS THE ANSWER

I

O Man! On the eve of the Holy Christmas, kneel down and pray even as the wise men from the East prayed beside the Baby Jesus. That was the greatest Message that Lord Jesus came amongst men to teach. Why have you forgotten so soon?

The breath has been given to you by the Lord, to be spent in prayer. Kneel down and pray: but let the prayer not cease when you rise. Prayer should be lifelong; and your life should be one long prayer.

There are no problems that cannot be dissolved by prayer: no suffering that cannot be allayed by prayer; no difficulties that cannot be surmounted by prayer; and no evil that cannot be overcome by prayer. Prayer is communion with God. Prayer is the miracle by which God's power flows into human veins. Therefore, kneel down and pray.

Greet the dawn of the day, and bid adieu to the setting sun with a prayer of thankfulness; first for a fresh day granted and last for His Grace received. Thus shall your life be blessed and thus will you radiate His Blessings to all around you.

When the storms of war and unrest gather around you, kneel down and pray. Remember the words of Abraham Lincoln, the greatest architect of freedom: "I have been driven many times to my knees by the overwhelming conviction that I had nowhere else to go. My own wisdom and that of all about me, seemed insufficient for the day." When the wisdom of politicians and social leaders fails, kneel down and pray: for a pair of praying hands are mightier than rulers of state and winners of battle. At this critical hour in human history, it is prayer alone that can pave the way for peace. Naught else is of any avail.

When, within your bosom rage the storms of lust and anger, vanity and viciousness, kneel down and pray. For, the Lord and He alone hath power over the elements. In thy supplication is thy strength. You will be filled with His Blessings, protected by His Grace, shielded by His Mercy and spurred on the Path of Righteousness by His Divine Will.

Therefore, kneel down and pray. Not, for earthly goods nor for heavenly pleasures, but, for His Grace, "Thy will be done, My Lord! I want nothing," shall be thy prayer. For you know not what is good for you, and you may be asking for trouble and praying for perdition. Pray for His Grace. Pray that His Righteousness might descend on the soul of all men. Pray that His Light might illumine the heart of all the leaders of men, and the path of humanity to peace. Kneel down and pray for our Saviour to save the world from its own "misleaders."

May the blessings of Lord Jesus be with you all this Holy Christmas and for ever afterwards. May there be Peace and Goodwill throughout the world! Hail Jesus. Amen.

II

THE VOICE OF JESUS

Jesus, the Son of God, and Divine Messenger upon earth, is verily the Infinite Love, Compassion and the Saving Grace of the Almighty, descended amidst humanity in the radiant form of a glorious human personality, the like of which mankind has rarely seen. The Almighty Spirit manifested Itself as an embodied Being for the uplift of mankind enmeshed in the binding net of earthly existence. Jesus came with the heartening Message of

Hope to a humanity weighed down under the burden of its sinful, ungodly life of mere materialistic sin-pursuits. He came to show the direct and easy way of freeing oneself from the guilt and bondage of an undivine living and of attaining the Joy, Bliss and Blessedness of the glorious Divine Life in the Spirit, or Atman. He taught the gospel of a pure life, a life of perfect faith, childlike simplicity and innocence, selflessness and love of all beings. Jesus lived and preached the sublime doctrine of renunciation of Mammon, and worship of God.

Voice of Eternal Being

The Voice of Jesus is verily the Voice of the Eternal Being. Through Him is expressed the call of the Infinite to the finite, the Cosmic Being to the individual, the call of God to man. His Divine Voice is the same, therefore, as the Voice of the Vedas and the Upanishads, the Voice of the Koran, the Gurugranth Saheb, the Zend Avesta, the Dhammapada, and all such sacred scriptures of the great religions of the world. Fundamentally the gospel that He preached is at one with the gospel expounded through these holy books. It is the way of denying the flesh and asserting the Spirit. It is the way of crucifying the lower self to bring about a glorious Resurrection of the Spirit and the final Ascension unto the Infinitude and the Transcendence unto the Divine. It is no other than the Upanishadic path of rejecting Preyas and accepting the Sreyas, the negation of the Anatma and the living of the life in the Atman.

Jesus declares: "Ye cannot serve both God and Mammon." In other words, His teaching implies: "Detach. Attach." Detach yourself from material objects of this transient world. Attach yourself to the Eternal Spiritual treasure of Atman. Christ thus teaches us the great way of going beyond all sin and sorrow. His Sermon is that which leads us from the darkness of this worldly existence of birth, death, disease and pain, unto the everlasting Light of glorious Divine Consciousness. It takes us away from the unreality of empirical phenomena to the Eternal Verity of

Transcendental Being, from the limited mortal existence to Unlimited Life Immortal.

Who Jesus Was

The vital importance and the deep significance of Jesus and His Immortal teachings will become clear to us only when we consider who Jesus was and how He came into being. Jesus was not an ordinary human being. He was the Divine Power and Love incarnated upon this globe for a special divine purpose. His advent was in the nature of a fulfilment of the Divine Plan for this world-process. This will be seen from the very manner of His birth and its background. Even before He illumined this terrestrial globe by the radiance of His Divine Presence, His advent was proclaimed and preached and broadcast by a Chosen Man of God, whom we know as John the Baptist.

It came about thus. Zacharias the priest and his wife Elizabeth were a holy and pious couple of Judea. We are told how the Angel Gabriel appeared to the good old priest and announced that it is God's Will that a son be born to him. He was to be the one to herald the advent of the Divine Son of God and to prepare the people for receiving Him. This boy, thus mysteriously born through Divine dispensation, grew up into a Holy Man, who came to be known as John the Baptist, and to fulfil Angel Gabriel's prophecy he made ready "a people prepared for the Lord." He thus paved the way for Jesus's incarnation. Later when actually the sacred and blessed hour of the Lord's birth drew near, the Heavens proclaimed His Divinity by a great Light that guided wise sages and the chosen among the faithful to the place of the Lord's Nativity. Thus the Light of the world first shone through the darkness of this world of delusion and nescience.

The Way He Taught

The way in which Jesus lived and taught was simple, yet sublime. His mode of teaching was something extraordinary. Jesus was no academic scholar. He could lay claim to neither degrees nor doctorate. He was not a Pandit or a savant. He had not attained proficiency or mastery in any practical art or science. He did neither indulge in high-flown oratory nor deliver learned pulpit sermons. When He spoke, He spoke but shortly and His brief words were few. His sayings were short, pithy and almost aphoristic. But His words were vibrant with an extraordinary power that was not of this world. They were vital and aflamed. They burnt themselves into the depths of the very consciousness of His hearers. And the reason?

When Jesus spoke, His blessed words came from the depths of a limitless Love and an infinite Divine Compassion that thrilled and thrilled again with an all-consuming, powerful desire to do good to man, to serve, to help and to save. This compassion to purify, to raise and to save mankind verily constitutes the sacred Heart of Jesus the Christ. This Love enlivened His words with a Divine Force, which made them to be permanently enshrined in the hearts of the fortunate hearers of His own blessed times and no less of the millions who read them even to this day through the holy pages of the Sacred Bible.

Practical Spirituality

Jesus was absorbed in the task of showing unto mankind a way out of this mundane life and attaining Eternal Bliss. He came to save men from this ocean of birth-death existence and to take them across to the other shore of Immortal Life. Therefore He preached the gospel of practical spirituality. Leaving aside all abstruse philosophical theory and subtle intellectual researches, Jesus told man how he must live, what he must think, what he must feel, and what he must do. To do this he clothed even the highest truths of spiritual life with simple stories and parables, which even the common man in the street could easily grasp and comprehend. Couched in the form of simple parables, the deepest wisdom of spiritual life became expressed before man, through the sweet and blessed words of Divine Jesus. Innumerable are the divine admonitions of Christ. Even a consideration of a select few of them would help to throw a great deal of light upon the path towards the attainment of the spiritual goal.

"Sin No More"

As we consider the sublime life of the Saviour, one of the very first important spiritual truths revealed to us comes through one of the most moving incidents recorded in the Gospel. The compassionate Lord moving through the city street comes suddenly upon an angry crowd. He sees that they are all taken wrathful with a woman who was caught in the act of sin, and were about to punish her with death. At the approach of the Saviour, the hapless woman takes shelter at His feet, shedding tears of remorse. Jesus turns with His serene and yet compelling countenance upon the angry crowd and challenges them to lift a hand against this woman, saying, "let him among you who is without sin cast the first stone." There is silence. All angry voices die out. Fear enters the heart of the multitude. Dropping the stones and sticks, the crowd disappears. Jesus is left alone with the repentant sinner at His feet. He raises her up and sends her away saying "go and sin no more." In these few words He reveals to us the great Law of the Spiritual Realm, i.e, that the soul which repents sincerely, gets absolved of all sins and receives the blessings of the Divine Compassion. O man! learn ye that if you will aspire for the true Grace, you have but to turn away from your evil ways and resolve that you will "sin no more."

Ingress of Divine Blessing

Should you but take this step of turning away from the darkness of evil in life, and step towards the light of a pure and divine life, then indeed you do open yourself up for the ingress of the Lord's blessings. But if these blessings are to enter into your being and attain their fullness and bear fruit in the form of rich spiritual experience, then you must prepare your heart for their right and proper reception, just as a farmer prepares the soil fully for the seeds to germinate and develop into a rich harvest.

What important part the right and proper receptivity of the seeker plays in the progress of spiritual life is brought out in a beautiful parable by Jesus. One warm, sultry day in Caparnaum the Lord has spent a busy forenoon, preaching, teaching, healing, consoling, inspiring and instructing vast multitudes that had thronged around Him. Towards evening He walks upon the shore of the lake. There, too, the multitudes follow. They press upon Him and Jesus gets into a boat and rowing a few yards away from the shore anchors upon the water. From there He turns upon the eager gathering. In sweet accents His loving words come to them.

He tells them how a farmer scatters the seeds for his field, which is by the roadside. There is a strong breeze. Some of the seeds are blown away and fall by the roadside, where birds pick them up and they are lost. Some seeds fall upon dry, hard rocks. There they have no soil to take root in. They wither up in the sun and die. Yet others fall upon good soil but being in the midst of thorns and brambles, though the seeds sprout up and the young seedlings grow into small plants, they are choked by thorns and brambles, and finally die. And lastly, those seeds that have fallen into good soil grow, develop, flourish and turn into a rich harvest.

Even so, though the Lord in His Loving Mercy is scattering abroad the precious seeds of spiritual truths that are to bear a harvest of supreme bliss, yet, unfortunately, all do not benefit fully out of them. Some hearts are so much constantly preyed upon by desires and earthly passions (birds) that the blessings of the Lord are not allowed to remain there at all. Some hearts are so totally dry, being devoid of faith and devotion, that in them spiritual truths wither and perish, even as the seeds fallen upon rocks do. In some other good natures, seeds of spiritual life take root, and start to grow, but alas the harsh thorns of bad company, worldly association and impure and undivine environment, choke the young spiritual plant and destroy it.

It is only the fortunate ones, the sincere and earnest seekers who have rendered themselves eminently receptive to all spiritual influences and who have prepared their hearts fully by prayer, spiritual discipline and selfless service, that reap the maximum benefit from the blessings that are ever being conferred by the Lord upon all mankind through His Divine Messengers, the saints and sages and devotees of all times and climes and through the sacred scriptures of all the great religions of the world. Therefore, O aspirant, through Sadachara and Seva, through diligent practice of Yama-Niyama, through the acquisition of Sadhana Chatushtaya, prepare your inward being perfectly, if you wish to reap the glorious harvest of spiritual bliss.

Senses of Values

If you are to ask why indeed should one take so much pains to receive the spiritual seeds, the reply is given through a number of connected parables. They go to explain how unparalleled and peerless indeed is the precious treasure of spiritual realisation. It is far more than all the wealth and enjoyment of entire earth put together. For its sake, a wise man will gladly give up everything. It is like the hidden treasure suddenly uncovered by a man at the plough. Full of joy, he hides the secret until he has sold away all that he had in order to buy the particular field for himself. By this he obtains the treasure which he knows to be far superior to all his petty possessions. Or, imagine a merchant seeking the finest of pearls. Then one day he finds the most precious pearl he has ever seen. Recognising its worth, he sells away all his other pearls, gems and his entire business in order to buy this pearl beyond all price.

Spiritual experience alone it is that gives worth to other aspects of life. Without it the other experiences of life are as nothing. It is like a little bit of yeast which a baker puts into a large quantity of flour. This little bit leavens the whole of the flour. Then again, how does the man of awakened discrimination act in his dealing with the spiritual and the material aspects of life? He knows which is good and which is useless. Therefore, he rejects the material and embraces the spiritual, just as a fisherman having drawn a net full of fish from the sea, keeps the good ones alone and casts away the bad ones back into the sea. The proper sense of values is revealed in this parable. You are told of your duty towards that which is worthy and that which is worthless. Know therefore the rare worth of the spiritual ideal. The seeker should be ready and willing to cast away all unspiritual things and to firmly adhere to the spiritual aim of life.

Be Not Heedless

In seeking to work out the spiritual ideal, one should be ever ready to accept all opportunities that the Lord puts before him for gathering spiritual experience. If he fails to do so, the blessings of God may be withheld from him. "Beware" says Jesus through His effective parable of the rich man and his feast. The rich man prepares a great and delicious feast and sent his servants to bring his friends to dine. But they all made excuses for not coming. Each one had some personal preoccupation or other—one his newly bought land, another his oxen, a third his young wife, and so on. When the rich man heard these excuses, he was displeased. "Go into the city streets," he ordered his servants, "and bring in the poor, the crippled and the blind." When there was yet room, he ordered "go beyond the city into the highways and the hedges and make all the outcasts and the destitute to come to the feast. Those who rejected my invitation shall never taste of my banquet." Even so, when opportunities for spiritual gain are offered, let one not commit the great blunder of rejecting them, for, later on, one will have to lament over the great gain that one deliberately bypassed and missed by one's neglect and heedlessness.

Need for Vigilance

Lastly, we come to the beautiful parable of the wise and the foolish bridesmaids, through which Jesus teaches how if we wish to avail of all spiritual opportunities, we need to be most alert and ever vigilant. Out of ten bridesmaids who fell asleep while waiting for the bridegroom, five were wise and they carried spare oil for their lamps, but five were foolish and they did not. So when they were suddenly called upon the groom's arrival, the lamps of the foolish maidens were out, but the wise ones who had kept the lamps burning bright readily went to the joyous marriage function. But the others were too late and were thus excluded from the rejoicing. So you must ever keep watch, for you never know when the auspicious hour of spiritual blessedness comes.

Thus, through all these beautiful and wise parables, the Lord Jesus taught the valuable lessons of truth, repentance, receptivity, renunciation, ready surrender and ever-alert spiritual vigilance to the seekers upon the path of Yoga and Self-realisation. He taught to us the great lesson of *uttishthata jagrata prapya varannibodhata.* Thus He lived and taught nearly twenty centuries ago. Thus the Light shone and illumined, and then entered into His Apostles through whom it later spread and enveloped the entire earth.

May all pray to the Blessed Lord Jesus, the Christ, to illumine our inmost being with the Light of His lofty Divine Presence and to graciously bestow upon all the Bliss of Christ-Consciousness. May all humbly strive to follow in His footsteps, and thus rise from darkness into Eternal Light, from this unreal world of ephemeral phenomena into the Transcendental Reality of the Supreme Being. May all rise beyond this world of mortality and attain to Life Immortal! May the power of Divine Love and Grace lift all from this realm of pain and sorrow into the realm of Eternal Light and Everlasting Bliss! Hail to Jesus, Divinity Incarnate. Amen.

1957

CHRIST-SPIRIT MUST BE ACQUIRED

Nineteen and a quarter of a century ago, Jesus of Nazareth said: "But I say unto you, love your enemies, bless them that curse you, do good to them that hate you, and pray for them which despitefully use you, and persecute you, that ye may be the children of your Father which is in Heaven; for He maketh

His sun to rise on the evil and on the good, and sendeth rain on the just and on the unjust." True, it is only a superhuman spiritual aspirant that can live up to this teaching, but at no time was there a greater need than now to assimilate at least part of its spirit in international relations.

What may be the sublimest virtue for the spiritual aspirant may not, indeed, be applicable in the formulation of collective perspective or national attitude. But, when Jesus asked to love one's enemies He did not imply that one should debase oneself, forsake the dignity of human life, abandon the cherished ideals of freedom of mind and spirit, justice and truth, but stressed upon the vital fact of the failure of hatred, belligerency, truncheon diplomacy, preconditioning of attitude and dogmatic pressure-politics to solve the agonising problems that beset the world and, worst of all, surreptitiously encroach upon the life of the common man.

Indeed, if Jesus were alive today, he would have been no less relentless than any fair-minded individual in opposing the equation of good with evil, truth with untruth, justice with the debasement of the human spirit, democracy with totalitarianism. The truth of the unalterable preference is never in question; the determination to uphold the former when assailed by the latter is never in question; but it is the spirit with which one fructifies the ideals of truth, dignity of life, freedom and fairplay in their widest concept, and the means that one pursues to foster them, that are challenged. The question looming large over mankind is whether one is justified to recourse to the very means one is trying to counteract, if one has any right to fan up the flames of war and destruction while crusading for the ideals that are essentially positive through the negative means of belligerency-psychosis, whereby the security of man is menaced and his economic well-being undermined.

The need of the hour is one of searching of the heart, and inquiring: if a little more of goodwill, a measure of cooperation in widening the areas of agreement, a spirit of accommodation without sacrificing one's ideals, a feeling for common security and well-being of the people, could not pose a better prospect of peace; if a little broadening of one's vision of the material interests and the spiritual welfare of man, a little more of initiative towards the solution of problems, a degree of effort at understanding the other man's point of view and his difficulties could not give a wholesome promise of amity and fellowship; if a will to succeed and strength to accept the unavoidable reconciliation to co-existence without necessarily sacrificing one's conviction of the inevitable victory of the ideals of truth and love and freedom of the human spirit, could not substantially contribute to common good.

May the teachings of Jesus Christ guide everyone's life!

Chapter Five

PARABLES OF LORD JESUS

1. Parable of the Builders

A wise man built his house on firm foundation. He dug deep and laid the foundation on a rock. The house could then weather many a storm. The rains came. The waves broke on the rock. But the house was safe... because it was built on the rock.

A foolish man built his house on sand. The rains came. The wind blew. The floods rose. The walls of the house crumbled down and the loss was great. Even so:

He is a wise man who learns spiritual truths and lives up to them. His wisdom and his life are founded upon the firm rock of practice. His wisdom and his life are unshaken by whatever might happen. In weal or woe, in rain or shine, in honour or dishonour his wisdom is changeless and his life unperturbed.

But, he is a foolish man who listens to spiritual truths or studies them, but does not live up to them. His wisdom and his life rest upon the shifting sands of theoretical understanding. And misfortune in life, an ailment, a defeat, or an insult would make his wisdom crumble down, and his life a mess. They cannot stand.

Therefore, be like the wise man: learn and translate what you have learnt into daily life.

2. The Good Samaritan

A traveller from Jerusalem to Jericho had been waylaid by robbers. They had stripped him. They caused him bodily injury. They had taken away all he had. He was in a dying condition.

A priest passed that way. He saw the groaning man. But he had his own work to do perhaps! He went his way.

Then came a Levite. He, too, went his way, disregarding the cry of the unfortunate traveller.

There came a Samaritan that way. The Samaritans were a mixed race; the orthodox people considered it a sin to have anything to do with them. But the Samaritan, without the trace of ill-will, knelt before the traveller, rendered him first aid, dressed his wounds, mounted him on his own horse, took him to an inn, and provided for his comfortable stay till he got well.

Of the three who is good? Surely, the Samaritan. He is the Good Samaritan. To the man of compassion everyone in need is neighbour. To render whatever help one can to everyone in need is what is meant by the golden words *"love thy neighbour as thyself."*

3. Parable of the Unclean Spirit

The evil spirit leaves the house. It wanders through waterless regions. It finds no rest anywhere. It returns to the house again. In the meantime, the house had been swept clean! But, what does the evil spirit do? It goes out and brings seven other kindred spirits with it, to dwell in the house. Imagine the state of the house then! Is it not worse than it was before? Even so:

The evil nature of man temporarily leaves him some times. It is starved out; association with the wise, precepts of sages, etc., prevent the evil from manifesting itself. These forces of the divine sweep the house (the heart of man) clean of all dirt and impurity. This does not last long, however! The evil nature returns. And, how? Often, sevenfold.

O man, beware! Be eternally vigilant. Look out for the signs of the return of old evil nature. Nip it in the bud. You will then be safe.

4. The Rich Fool

There was a rich man whose land yielded a rich harvest during a certain year. But his barns were small. They could not accommodate all the grain. The rich man, however, wanted to store all the grain for his own use. He thought he could eat, drink and be merry... for he had plenty of material wealth. But God said to him: "O fool! Your soul is required tonight. Who will take the wealth you have thus hoarded?"

He passed away, without either enjoying the riches himself or having the satisfaction of giving them away to the needy. Such is the fate of all greedy people.

O rich fool! You are only the trustee of the wealth the Lord has entrusted to you. Share what you have with the poor and the needy. When your soul departs from the body, it will find that the Lord is well pleased with it; for the wealth of the Lord bestowed upon you had been nicely shared by you with His other children. *Hoard not wealth.*

5. The Prerequisites

One who desires to build a tower should first sit down, calculate the cost and find out if he has enough to complete the work. Otherwise—if he foolishly embarks on the task without first drawing up the plan and acquiring the raw materials—he will not be able to complete the work and would make himself the laughing stock of the public.

Similarly, a king going to wage war with another king, would first take counsel with his ministers and calculate the strength of his own army, compared to the strength of the enemy's army. If he does not equip himself properly, then he would have to beg for the enemy's terms of peace! Even so:

When a seeker embarks on the life divine, he ought to think well and ponder the prerequisites of spiritual life. He ought to equip himself with dispassion, discrimination and a true spirit of renunciation. Or, he will be forced to stop short of his goal. He would be laughed at by the people.

Or, he might have to surrender himself to the undivine forces and suffer great spiritual downfall.

O spiritual aspirants! Take heed. Acquire first the Four Means to Salvation. Then you will have no cause for grief.

6. The Pharisee and the Tax Collector

Two men went up to a temple to pray. One was a Pharisee and the other a Tax Collector.

The Pharisee noticed the Tax Collector praying at a distance. So, he prayed within himself: "God, I thank Thee; for I am not like the other men, extortioners, unjust adulterers, not even like this Tax Collector. I have fasted twice a week, and I give tithes of all that I get."

The Tax Collector did not even raise his head, but beat his breast and prayed: "God, be merciful to me, a sinner."

God was pleased with the Tax Collector. For, in his heart was humility. The Pharisee was proud of his piety. And, the pride overshadowed all other virtues. Religious pride is dangerous. It is worse than material pride, pride of wealth, etc. Religious pride is the greatest obstacle to spiritual progress.

Be humble.

7. Parable of the Five Foolish Virgins

Ten virgins went to meet the bridegroom. They all had lamps in their hands. Five of them had taken extra oil with them. Five of them had not.

As they were waiting for the bridegroom, they slept. After a few hours, there was commotion; and the bridegroom was announced. The virgins woke up. The five that had extra oil were ready to go. The other five who had no extra oil said to the former five: "Please give us some of your oil; for our lamp is going out." But the five wise virgins refused, saying: "Then, we may not have enough for keeping even our lamps burning, till we reach him; you had better go to the bazaar and get some oil for yourselves." The five wise virgins went to meet the bridegroom. The five foolish ones, went to the bazaar to fetch oil. But before they could return, the door was closed and they could not enter and meet the bridegroom.

Similar is the case with the vigilant spiritual aspirant and the foolish man who indulges the senses. The former equips himself with the Four Means, acquires the wealth of God's Name and spiritual practices; and when the messengers of God come to take him away from this earth-plane, he is ready and fully equipped to meet the Lord. But the foolish sensuous man wastes his life here, does not care to acquire spiritual wealth; and the lamp of his life goes out before he could make any progress towards the Lord. He returns to the bazaar—to this world of birth and death.

O Man! Be ever prepared. Live this moment as though it is your last moment on this earth and acquire the maximum spiritual wealth here and now.

8. Parable of the Two Sons

A man went to his first son and said: "Son, go and work in the vineyard today." But the son answered, "I will not," but later on he repented and went to work.

Then he went to the second son and said the same thing. He readily said: "I will." But he did not go.

Which of the two did the father's will? Surely, the former. So, the father was highly pleased with him.

It often happens like that in the world. God sends His Messengers to redeem mankind. They come and call out to the people to walk the path of righteousness and to return to God. The sinners at first refuse; but soon they realise their folly and quickly return to the God-path. But the hypocrite readily agrees and promises; but does nothing more than lip-service to righteousness and divine life.

God is more pleased with even the sinner who, in the words of the Gita, resolves to turn to the path of divine life: for, the Lord promises, quickly he becomes a pure soul *(Kshipram bhavati dharmatma)* and attains to peace. The hypocrite who pretends to be righteous but who does not do the Will of God, remains behind.

Let your action speak.

9. Parable of the Importunate Friend

A man was asleep with his children. A friend of his was in urgent need of three loaves of bread to feed his guests. It was past midnight. The friend knocked at the door of the sleeping man. There was no answer at first; but he knocked again. He said: "O friend, kindly give me three loaves of bread. I have nothing to feed my guests with." But the man within the house replied: "Do not bother me now. My children are sleeping with me; and it is past midnight." But the friend persisted and knocked again. And, the man had to get up and oblige the friend.

Even so one has to persevere in spiritual practices, in righteousness, in charity, in prayerfulness. There is an inexhaustible magazine of power within everyone; but this is asleep, as it were. The spiritual aspirant knocks at the door of this Power; he prays for three loaves of bread—Immortality, Eternal Bliss and Perennial Peace. At first it seems as though his prayer has fallen only on deaf ears. If he despairs then, and gives up his prayer, he will gain nothing. But the wise aspirant knocks again. There is a response from within as it were: but it is a negative one. His own evil tendencies, past evil deeds, and internal imperfections deny him the great gift of the Three Loaves. The man is not disheartened even then. He knocks again: he wins the prize. The Power is fully awakened and he gains what he sought after.

Ask. It will be given you.
Seek. You will find.
Knock. It will be opened to you.

10. The Parable of the Sower
(In the words of the Holy Bible)

Again He began to teach beside the sea. And a very large crowd gathered about Him, so that He got into a boat and sat in it on the sea; and the whole crowd was beside the sea on the land. And He taught them many things in parables, and in His teaching He said to them: "Listen! A sower went forth to sow.

And as he sowed, some seed fell along the path, and the birds came and devoured it. Other seed fell on rocky ground, where it had not much soil, and immediately it sprung up since it had no depth of soil; and when the sun rose it was scorched, and since it had no root it withered away. Other seed fell among thorns and the thorns grew up and choked it, and it yielded no grain. And other seeds fell into good soil and brought forth grain, growing up and increasing and yielding thirty-fold and sixty-fold and a hundred-fold." And He said, "He who has ears to hear, let him hear."

And He said to them, "Do you not understand this parable? How then will you understand all the parables? The sower sows the word, and these are the ones along the path, where the word is sown; when they hear, Satan immediately comes and takes away the word which is sown in them. And these in like manner are the ones sown upon rocky ground, who, when they hear the word, immediately receive it with joy; and they have no root in themselves, but endure for a while; then, when tribulation or persecution arises on account of the word, immediately they fall away. And others are the ones sown among thorns; they are those who hear the word, but the cares of the world, the delight in riches, and the desire for other things, enter in and choke the word, and it proves unfruitful. But those that were sown upon the good soil are the ones who hear the word and accept it and bear fruit, thirty-fold and sixty-fold and a hundred-fold.

Mark: 4: 1-9, 13-20

11. Parable of the Lost Sheep

A man had a hundred sheep. He had taken them out for grazing. As he was returning, he found that one of them was missing. He immediately left the ninety-nine and ran searching for that missing sheep. He knew the ninety-nine would safely reach home. He found the missing sheep. He rejoiced and put it on his shoulders. As soon as he reached home, he called out to his neighbours: "Rejoice with me, for I have found my sheep which was lost."

Even so the man-of-God is intent on reforming the sinner and bringing him over to the path of divine life, though this means a lot of hard toil for him. He knows that those that are righteous will reach the Home—God—safely. When even one sinner is reclaimed, the gods and the Maharshis rejoice.

12. Parable of the Talents

A man going on a journey called his servants and entrusted to them his property; to one he gave five talents, to another two, to another one, to each according to his ability.

After a long time, the master returned and wanted to settle the accounts. The servant who received five talents had traded with them and made five more. He placed these ten before the master and explained what he had done. The master was highly pleased, and said: "Well done, a good and faithful servant; you have been faithful over a little, I will set you over much: enter into the joy of your master." Similarly, the servant who had received two talents placed four before the master and received similar praise. But the servant to whom the master had given one talent returned it to him, saying that he knew the master was strict in his dealings and since he (the servant) did not want to lose the talent, he had hidden it safely away and brought it back now. The master was annoyed and said: "You wicked and slothful servant! You ought to have invested the money with the bankers." To others he said: "So, take the talent from him and give it to him who has ten. And, cast the worthless servant into the outer darkness."

The significance of this parable is obvious. By God's Grace man acquires a certain amount of piety, charitable disposition, spiritual leanings, etc. These virtues must be augmented by constant exercise. Life, human birth, is a golden opportunity, to do so. He who thus augments virtue becomes the Lord's beloved and enjoys Bliss with Him in the Kingdom of Heaven. He who wastes this life, and does not make any use of his innate virtue, loses even that and comes to grief.

Be positively and vigorously good and righteous.

13. The Parable of the Prodigal Son

The younger son approached his father and said: "Father, give me here and now, my share of the property." And, as soon as the father had done so, the young man went away to a distant country. Soon the money was spent in luxury. A famine struck the country. The young man was very miserable. He thought of his father and said to himself: "I shall go to him and tell him—Father, I have sinned against heaven and before you; I am no longer worthy to be called your son; treat me as one of your hired servants." Even before he had reached his home his father had seen him from a distance. He rushed forward to embrace the son who pleaded to be treated as a hired servant. But the father had the best clothes brought for the son, all ornaments, and the best food. The return of the young man was celebrated as a festival. The elder son on returning home from the field was told of the festivity; he was angry. "Lo," he said "these many years I have served you; and I never disobeyed your command; yet you never gave me a kid, that I might make merry with my friends. But when this son of yours, who has devoured your living with harlots, you killed for him the fatted calf!" But the father replied: "Son, you are always with me, and all that is mine is yours. It was fitting to make merry and be glad, for this your brother was dead, and is alive; he was lost, and is found."

This parable, too, has the same moral as the Parable of the Lost Sheep. The wicked man—his life and his energy are also the gift of God—squanders his life and his energy in evil ways. He comes to grief. Disease and old age assail him. Then he returns to God. The celestials and saints rejoice exceedingly when such a one returns to the path of righteousness: for, a wayward man has been reclaimed to the path of Truth.

14. Parable of the Hidden Treasure

"The Kingdom of Heaven is like treasure hidden in a field, which a man found and covered up; then in his joy he goes and sells all that he has and buys that field."

This is a beautiful small parable pregnant with spiritual significance.

The Bliss of the Soul, the Peace that passeth understanding, is the hidden treasure. It is in the very innermost recesses of man's heart. It is revealed to man by the preceptor, the master, the Guru.

Overjoyed at this spiritual initiation by the Guru, the spiritual aspirant sells all that he has. He renounces the little pleasures of the world. But all the time he keeps the initiation well "covered." He does not boast about it and about the hidden treasure. He keeps silent; and works silently to possess it.

After renouncing the world and its petty joys, he purchases the field—spiritual life, divine life, service of the Guru and study of scriptures—and now he comes in possession of the hidden treasure, too.

15. Parable of the Seed and the Harvest

"The Kingdom of God is as if a man should scatter seed upon the ground, and should sleep and rise night and day; and the seed should sprout and grow, he knows not how. The earth produces of itself, first the blade, then the ear, then the full grain in the ear. But when the grain is ripe, at once he puts in the sickle, because the harvest has come." —Mark 4: 26-29.

All the actions of man are like the seeds sown; in the Kingdom of God they germinate and grow into plants; in due time they ripen and produce fruits; and when they are ripe, man harvests them in a subsequent birth. *As you sow so shall you reap.* Mysterious is the law of Karma.

Or

Man repeats the Names of the Lord. He meditates and engages himself in spiritual practices. His piety, righteousness and charity are the seeds that are sown in the Kingdom of God. In due time, they yield the delightful fruits of wisdom and

God-realisation. The harvest is immortality and eternal bliss. The spiritual growth is not apparent; but the harvest is unmistakably evident.

Chapter Six
A SYMPOSIUM
CHRISTMAS—ITS SPIRITUAL MEANING

(Sri Swami Sivananda)

Christmas is known to all men the world over historically as the memorable day of the birth of Jesus, the Saviour. Though it is true that Christmas is thus celebrated as the day of the advent of Christ into this world, yet it also symbolises a very deeply significant truth of the spiritual life. Jesus Christ lived and symbolised Divine Consciousness. He is the very personification of Divinity. He was born at a time when ignorance, superstition, greed, hatred and hypocrisy prevailed upon the land. The rulers were arrogant and unrighteous. The people were avaricious, indolent and heedless. Purity was forgotten. Morality was neglected. They were more intent upon worshipping Mammon than adoring God. There was no idealism.

In the midst of these conditions, Christ was born and He worked a transformation in the lives of people. He gave a new and a spiritual turn to the lives of man. There came a change upon the land. People started upon a new way of life. Thus a new era dawned for the world.

Those conditions of darkness, impurity and materialism that prevailed before the coming of Christ signify to you the inner state of the seeker's personality before discrimination had dawned upon him and before a spiritual awakening had taken place. In that period the seeker has no thought of God or higher spiritual life. He is immersed in the pursuit of the material things of this external physical world. He is the slave of his senses. He has no spiritual ideal in life. He is desire-ridden. Arrogance, avarice and sensuality characterise his personality. He lives a life of lust, anger, greed, deluded attachment, pride and jealousy.

If this state of things must cease and the seeker must enter into a new life of spiritual aspiration, purity and devotion, then the Christ-spirit must take its birth within his heart. That is the real Christmas when the Divine element begins to express itself in the heart of the man. From then onward, light begins to shine where darkness was before. Ignorance gives place to the beginning of wisdom. Impurity is replaced by purity. Hatred ceases and love begins to blossom forth.

In his innermost core, man is essentially Divine. But upon this field of human personality two forces keep acting. They are the forces of good and evil, of light and of darkness. The Divine and the undivine both operate in the human consciousness of man. To completely overcome and eradicate the undivine elements and to fully manifest the supreme Divine element in all its radiant light and glory is to be achieved only through the living of the Christ-life, in the utmost faithful detail. This is spiritual life. This is Yoga. This is Sadhana (spiritual practice). This is the method of Self-realisation. This is the great Path which leads us to Immortality, Supreme Bliss and Eternal Peace.

If the Christ-life is to be lived, first of all, the child-Christ has to be born in us. Then only the real spiritual life commences for the aspirant. The first manifestation of the Divine urge in the form of spiritual aspiration and the recognition of the spiritual ideal signifies the birth of the infant Jesus within the seeker's being. From hence starts the living of the Christ-life in all its spiritual details of sublime purity, faith in Divinity, mercy, compassion, love, selflessness, desirelessness, prayerfulness, etc. Hence starts the life of earnest Yoga and Sadhana, of self-restraint and simplicity, of unbroken serenity and peace, balance of mind, unflinching courage in the face of all oppositions and perfect dedication to the worship of God through the service of man. This is the spiritual implication within of the Christmas that is celebrated without.

With the advent of this Christ-spirit within the heart of the seekers, all human desires come to an end and they are replaced by pure higher Divine aspiration. Spirituality overcomes materialism. You break free from your slavery to the senses. You begin to live a new life, a divine life of purity, love, renunciation, humility, non-attachment and selflessness. Your life becomes sublime like the life of Christ. You begin to live a life of complete faith and dependence upon God. You always think of God, talk of Him and live for Him. Helping others becomes a real joy to you. You become a living witness of the Divine. All your life's activities flow towards God.

Here a very small, but very beautiful, point of deep significance is to be noted without fail. It reveals a deep spiritual Law. It is the time and the manner of the birth of the Lord upon the holy Christmas day. Jesus Christ was not born in a grand palace. He was not born to very wealthy or learned parents. Also He was not born in the full blaze of day-light with the knowledge of all men. Jesus Christ was born in a simple lowly place, a corner of a stable. He was born to humble and poor parents, who had nothing to boast about, except their own spotless character and holiness. Also He was born in the darkness in the obscure hour of midnight, when no one even knew about it, except a few Divinely blessed people.

The above point of deep significance tells you that the spiritual awakening comes to the seeker, who is perfectly humble and "meek" and "poor in spirit." The quality of true humility is one of the indispensable fundamentals. Then we find simplicity, holiness and the renunciation of all desire for worldly wealth and pride of learning. Thirdly, even as Christ was born unknown to the world and in the obscurity of darkness, even so, the advent of the Christ-spirit takes place in the inwardness of man when there is total self-effacement, self-abnegation. Where self-aggrandisement and vanity abide, there the descent of Divinity cannot occur, for these expressions of egotism are ever a bar to the unfoldment of the Divine consciousness. Empty thyself and I shall fill thee—is the Divine admonition of the Lord. The Kingdom of Heaven within is for the lowly in spirit. Thus, true humility and self-effacement are the beautiful harbingers, the dawnlights, as it were, that herald the break of the joyous new day, the advent of the new era of a life in Spirit. When they appear within you, then the holy Christmas takes place. There is a new birth then.

This is the birth into a Divine Life. It was the secret of this birth that centuries ago the Lord Jesus sweetly explained to the good Nicodemus. The good man did not quite understand what precisely Christ meant when He taught that a man must be born again if he is to attain the Kingdom of God. "How can this be?" Nicodemus asked. Then it was that Christ explains that this birth is inward, not of the body, but in the Spirit. Such inner spiritual birth is essential if the Supreme is to be attained, if true bliss is to be experienced. Rejoicing takes place only when Christmas has come.

O humanity! O modern age! Hearken to this significant inner message of Christmas. May the true implication of the Divine Christ Personality dawn upon your hearts! Realise fully that so long as the thirst for Mammon and the arrogance of power infects the nature of man, so long the Christ-spirit of peace, blessedness and true happiness cannot enter into your life. When Christmas is being celebrated all over the Continent and in England, America and in the entire Christian world, may this be borne in mind that, "unless ye be born again, ye cannot enter into the Kingdom of Heaven," and that unless the simplicity and the purity of heart of the little children come to indwell the hardened, unregenerate nature of the modern man, the advent of the Divine Grace as peace, prosperity, universal well-being and concord are indeed far, far away. As with the individual, even so with the nations of the world, the fundamentals of true faith, true charity, genuine humility and a spiritual rebirth alone can usher in true bliss and brotherhood upon this earth. It is when such a transformation occurs in the nations of men and it is when they renounce their policies of hatred and greed that the modern world will truly enjoy the blessings of the real, universal Christmas. Then will be the advent of the Blessed Christ into this despairing world. Till then Christmas will be but a travesty of the real glory of the Lord's advent. Be born again and live anew, O World of Today! May the bliss and radiance of the Lord's advent permeate the earth!

But seekers, mark this! When Divinity is to manifest, welcome it with open arms. Do not be so engrossed in the world and deny place to the Lord. At His blessed advent the land was so engrossed in counting men and reckoning of money that the inns and houses of Bethlehem were so crowded out that there was hardly any place left to receive the Lord. The census and the taxation signify the soul's bondage to and preoccupation in earthly human relationships and attachments and its engrossment with lucre. Let the aspirant beware of these two vital mistakes. Turning away inwardly from all pursuit of earthly wealth and overcoming all attachment, be thou ever fully receptive to the expression of the Divine Spirit within.

Beloved seekers! Usher in now the real and spiritual Christmas within your being. Become desireless. Conquer egoism. Become embodiments of true humility. Develop meekness and lowliness of spirit by humble surrender unto the Lord. Be courageous to overcome all obstacles. Joyously renounce Mammon. Welcome the descent of the Light of Grace within. Rejoice in the advent of the Divine. Thus celebrate the Christmas that ultimately leads you on to the glorious climax of Transfiguration, Resurrection and Ascension. Be crowned with Divine glory. Attain immortality, perfect freedom and be for ever steeped in infinite bliss. Through Christmas realise the Christ-consciousness and the radiant light of Atmic (divine) Wisdom. Amen.

'THY KINGDOM COME'

(Sri Swami Chidananda)

My heart's love and adoration, my countless crores of humble and devout prostrations again and again at the blessed feet of Lord Jesus, Divinity incarnate upon earth, for the redemption of man and for showing man the path to supreme blessedness, bliss and Highest Atmic Illumination. Worshipful salutations to Jesus the Christ, the Son of God, the radiant exemplar of a Divine Life in this world. Blessed indeed am I, a humble servant of His sacred feet to have this privilege of dwelling upon His sublime Personality and life.

Nearly twenty centuries ago, upon the holy and auspicious day of Christmas, the Grace and Compassion of the Almighty Being descended here upon this earth in the form of a Divine Being, Whom we now adore as Lord Jesus the Christ. He is God's Love embodied in human form. The glory of Divinity shone through this wondrous Personality. That solemn night a great stellar light illumined the eastern skies to herald the descent of this Parama-Jyoti, this Divine Ray of the Supreme Light of lights, the Atman, which was to illumine this terrestrial globe for all times. Ah! how blessed indeed, most blessed indeed is that great day when this earth became hallowed by the sacred presence of this Divine incarnation. Rejoice, O humanity, rejoice that you have this Supreme Light that illuminates and guides you upon the path to the Blissful Realm beyond all sorrow, pain and mortality. Rejoice that you have a Divine Friend, Philosopher and Master, who teaches you through His sublime life precept and personality, the secret of Supreme Blessedness.

Lord Jesus came to teach us the way to attain the joy and perfection of the Divine Kingdom. He lived and taught us to find out the Kingdom of Heaven that is within ourselves. His inspiring call to man was for the renunciation of the low and petty things of this perishable, physical world and to strive for the attainment of the lofty spiritual ideal of Divine Perfection, perennial Bliss and Immortal Existence. He taught that the realisation of the Atman is far, far more than the entire wealth of all the world put together. 'Attain first the Kingdom of Heaven and ye shall have all things added unto you.' 'What availeth it a man if he gains the whole world, but loses his Soul?' For, this indeed is to be known that the Atman is the Supreme Treasure more precious than all earthly treasure. The Atman is imperishable, everlasting, supremely Perfect and of the nature of infinite Bliss. Having come upon this earth, abandon all foolish pursuit after perishable objects of this mortal realm and seek the imperishable, everlasting, the Supreme. Herein lies blessedness. Herein lies bliss. Thus taught Jesus.

Therefore seek ye first the Kingdom of God. Live like Christ. Abandon completely all the trifling objects of this transitory world. Renounce all desire and follow the Lord. "Unless a man forsakes all" said Jesus, "he cannot be my disciple." Remember His admonition to the rich young ruler, "There is one thing more—sell all you have and give to the poor. Then take up your Cross and follow Me." Then again, "No man who looks back once he has put his hand to the plough is fit for God's Kingdom." Renounce everything and thou shalt attain all.

By His life the Blessed Lord has taught us that to die in the lower life of the flesh is verily to be reborn into the glorious life in the spirit. We have His significant saying, "He who loses his life for My sake shall find it." To annihilate the impure ego, to eradicate all desires, to root out lust, destroy all falsehood and give up all attachments of the flesh is the way to blossom into the Life Spiritual. The life of Tapasya and Titiksha, of self-denial, sacrifice, hardship and penance is the taking up of the Cross in order to follow Him unto glory. Humility, righteousness, compassion, purity are the portals to the Blissful Kingdom of Heaven.

Let us be with the Lord for just a while and let us see how He taught this holy path to blessedness and glory. It is on a holy Sabbath day. The place is blessed Capernaum. The Lord has preached and taught in the Synagogue and later repaired to Peter's house. It is evening. Great crowds of all manner of people have gathered about Him. Jesus is blessing, healing, curing and consoling. The crowd increases. Seeing the multitudes, behold Jesus going up into a mountain, the people closely following Him, and there He turns round and addresses them. There standing on the crest of the Mount, behold how He looks thrilling, inspiring and radiant, framed against the crimson and gold of the glorious evening sky. Spiritual brilliance shines from His face. His entire Being is radiant with an ethereal Light. And thus He speaks to them all and delivering Himself in sweet accents full of compassion He says unto them:

Blessed are the poor in spirit: for theirs is the Kingdom of Heaven.

Blessed are they that mourn: for they shall be comforted.

Blessed are the meek: for they shall inherit the earth.

Blessed are they which do hunger and thirst after righteousness: for they shall be filled.

Blessed are the merciful: for they shall obtain mercy.

Blessed are the pure in heart: for they shall see God.

Blessed are the peacemakers: for they shall be called the children of God.

Blessed are they which are persecuted for righteousness's sake: for theirs is the Kingdom of Heaven.

Blessed are ye, when men shall revile you and persecute you, and shall say all manner of evil against you falsely for My sake.

Rejoice, and be exceeding glad: for great is your reward in heaven: for so persecuted they the prophets which were before you.

And after this manner you should pray:
"Our Father which art in heaven,
Hallowed be Thy name.
Thy kingdom come,
Thy will be done,
On earth as it is in heaven.
Give us this day our daily bread;
And forgive us our debts,
As we forgive our debtors;

And lead us not into temptation,
But deliver us from evil.
For Thine is the kingdom,
The power and the Glory,
For ever and ever, Amen."

This is His Sermon, the Sermon that shall endure as long as man is. In it we have the essence of all scriptures and all the religions. Herein you have the heart of the Vedas and the Upanishads, expounding the royal path to Godhead, by dying to the lower self, to live the Divine Life of utter egolessness, humility, purity, righteousness, compassion, devotion and surrender. Ah! Blessed Gospel, how greatly blessed this world would be if Thou wert enshrined in the hearts of all men!

Jesus has spoken. It is for us to act. The Light shines and it illumines the path. It is for you, and for all of us, to tread along upon the path and uttering "Thy Kingdom come" to enter joyously into the Realm Divine. 'Give us this day our daily bread' is really a prayer for the spiritual food, the Divine Manna of Sadhana Sakti and Yoga. 'Deliver us from evil' is not indeed so much external, but rather a prayer to safeguard us from the Shadripus (lust, anger, greed, deliberate attachment, pride and jealousy) and save us from Maya, the Supreme Illusion. To live in the spirit of the Sermon on the Mount is to imitate and to follow Christ in the truest manner. To follow Him is to ascend into blessedness. He who follows Jesus faithfully shall ascend from the unreal to the Real, from darkness into Eternal Light, from mortality to Immortality. If you live in the spirit of the Lord's Sermon, then your prayer 'Our Father Which art in Heaven, THY KINGDOM COME' shall be answered forthwith and the Kingdom of Heaven will be manifest to you here and now. Joy, peace and blessedness will prevail in your life.

Sweet Jesus, Blessed Lord, grant this slave's humble prayer that Thy Presence within the heart may inspire him to follow in Thy glorious footsteps. May we all be blessed with Thy Grace to turn away from this fleeting world of vanishing names and forms and to seek first the Kingdom of God! Give us the strength to be man and live like man with the true heroism of Inner Spirit. May we carry our Crosses with courage and joy and face life as You have shown us to face it! Grant that we may lead the Divine Life and attain the true goal of Divine Perfection!

Glory be to Lord Jesus, the Prince of purity and peace, the Messenger of mercy, the Lord of Love, Divine Deliverer of mankind, God incarnate, Who dwelt in flesh and showed by His life the path to perennial Bliss and Spiritual Glory! Hail Jesus, hail Mary, Mother of God! Hail Almighty, Thy Kingdom come!!

A SACRAMENTAL LIFE

(Sri Swami Krishnananda)

Jesus came to bear witness to the light Transcendent. Saints incarnate themselves by the behest of the Supreme Father of the universe to raise humanity from ignorance, error and sin to the life Righteous and Beatific. Saint Tukaram has said, "We live in Vaikuntha, but we come down to help humanity." The All-powerful spiritual law that governs the universe manifests itself in infinite forms to establish itself in the realm of manifestation. Each form thus manifested bears witness to the Light Eternal. The suffering of the son of God, Christ, is a brilliant example of how the incarnated symbol of the eternal bears witness to its source. There is a great meaning implied in the suffering of the Saint, whether it is deliberately imposed upon himself by himself in the form of ascetic denial or it is imposed on him by external agencies. He that loves the world loves not the Father, and he that dies for the sake of the son of God, truly lives. The implication of all this is that to establish the righteousness of God in this mundane realm and to bear witness to the undying law that is supermundane, the son of God, the great Saint, lives the life of an abnegation of conformity to the customs and rules of the deluded earth and affirms with all force the non-earthly character of the ideal life. To die to the narrow life of the earth is to live in the peace that passeth all understanding.

Christ has said that he came here to obey the commands of his Father, to do the Will of his Father. And he has also said that the heaven of the Father is within all. This means that the life of the Saint is a sacrifice done for the sake of asserting the spiritual law of that which is within all. The All which is within everyone is the true Father of humanity and all beings. The life of man is meant to demonstrate the goodness and the love, the wisdom and the truth which is his own origin. The assertion of the righteousness of the universal life which is an expression of the great Father in Heaven requires therefore the assertion of all the unifying forces in this world of diversity. The life of the saint is a sacrament, a holy act, a divine worship. Suffering is inevitable to the saint who is the son of God, for, as the Christ has said, the one that is of God has no place to rest. Nothing here can satisfy the infinite impulse to be righteous and to do the righteous. From birth to crucifixion the life of Jesus has been a saga of the process of self-perfection. The incidents in his life represent the microcosmic as well as the macrocosmic changes that take place in the history of the evolution of the universe towards Self-realisation in the existence of God.

Every phase of life is a necessary moment in the continued endeavour of the universe to recognise itself in Self-consciousness and unity of powers. Though the life of every person is indicative of the nature of the entire evolution of that individual, past as well as future, resulting in the experience of perfection, the life of Jesus, as well as of Sri Krishna, is a direct illustration of the conscious and systematic movement of the consciousness from its rudimentary individual state to the fully blossomed attainment of the infinite Godhead. If spiritual effort consciously and deliberately exerted can be defined as the process of the compression of the entire evolutionary play into one life, the life of Jesus can be said to be a concrete representation in picturesque forms of this drama of evolution.

Jesus reveals himself in this world at a time when the king of the country strives his best to oppose him. Jesus has to be protected by being taken to a distant place. He grows up under mysterious circumstances and begins to preach the gospel of Divine Life. He is opposed again, tempted in several ways, charged with guilt, tried in court, found fault with, and crucified.

The soul of man, in the same way, begins to peep out through its material vestures when it finds itself hemmed in by disturbing powers of the physical and the mental world. The spiritual spark has to be saved from being extinguished completely. This is the preliminary step in the practice of Yoga. Sometimes the soul loses itself in a dark night and, later mysteriously emerges out of the same to assert itself with its full dignity and power. It begins to establish its law in all that it experiences and while doing so the powers of the manifested universe come in conflict with its super-normal behaviour. The individual soul with its new alignment with the Supreme Self finds itself persecuted by the natural forces of the world. It is tempted vehemently, tried in all possible ways and declared unfit for a natural life in the world. It finds it impossible to live at the same time both in the conscious realm of God and the lusty world of man. It abandons itself to the Will of the Supreme and for the sake of this beatific union with the Infinite it casts off its individuality and ceases to be an element in the changing and objective plane of death, where the passions drag one away from God.

The teachings of Christ constitute the essential principles that regulate the course of the spiritual aspirant in his quest of the great ideal. Faith is the fundamental key to success in spiritual life. Christ has also warned people that many may come in his garb but may not be real teachers. One has to be aware of these deceitful ones and lay one's trust in the true teacher, the Christ. The power of faith is such that, as Christ puts it, even a grain of it can move a mountain hence. Thought of food and raiment is not to become the burden of the aspirant. It is the instruction of Jesus that God knows more than man and that He knows how to protect man. The one duty of a person is to come to Him alone for rest, light and salvation. But "not everyone that sayeth unto me, Lord, Lord, shall enter into the kingdom of heaven; but he that doeth the will of my Father which is in heaven." It is not verbal humility and devotion but sincere feeling of dedication and surrender that can take one to God. Spiritual effort has its aim not in public worship, adoration in the streets and beating of drums, but silent sacrifice and intense feeling of union with the One without a second. "Blessed are they which do hunger and thirst after righteousness, for they shall be filled. Blessed are they that mourn, for they shall be comforted. Blessed are they which are persecuted for righteousness' sake, for their's is the kingdom of heaven." God reveals Himself to man not until he becomes ready to sacrifice his life for His sake.

The greatness of the devotee of God is like a sweet fragrance which makes itself felt by all, by its very presence. "They are the light of the world; a city that is set on a hill cannot be hid." The spiritual essence that constitutes the core of a person in union with Divine, reveals itself, of its own accord, without any kind of effort on the part of the person who is the medium of that revelation. The sun does not proclaim himself when he rises in the sky, but his very presence makes itself felt by those who have eyes to see and sense to feel. The owl does not know the sun, the blind does not see the light, the ignorant are not aware of the moving spirit of God that dwells in the tabernacle here and shines through the saint. The acts of Christ and his disciples are to be taken not in the sense of processes that have their end in the fulfilment of an individual wish, but as parts of cosmic movement tending to the establishment of God's glory in the universe.

The life of Christ is a veritable sacrament, an outward and visible sign of inward and spiritual grace that descends from the Sovereign of the universe. It is the unbounded love of God that came in flesh and suffered for the sins of humanity to raise the latter to the source of this love. Love and sacrifice are the key to open the door of immortality. Prayer, not for one's own salvation from pain, but for the redemption of others from the ignorance of the law of God, is the true form which love and sacrifice takes in the life virtuous. The miracles which Christ performed are indicative of the Omnipotence of Him for whose sake Christ came here. The mission of the life of Jesus is not merely to open the eyes of man to the light that shines beyond the dust of the earth, but also to hoist the banner of the kingdom of heaven on this very earth, by winning for righteousness victory over evil and the temptations of Satan. Life here is a blending of the relative laws of the earth and the absolute law of God. "Render unto Caesar the things which are Caesar's; and unto God the things that are God's." A development of the aspiration for the Spirit, in harmony with the rules that regulate the kingdom of God and the kingdom of the earth, is necessary in order that the aspirant may be free from the error of the over-emphasis of non-essentials and of neglect of essentials in this relative life. Man is God and brute crossed at one point, and so he has to transcend the brute by an intelligent application of the divine power within him to what is active in him as the undivine force.

Christ was a great realist when he stressed the importance of kindness, love, service and worship of God as the Father in heaven. He was a great idealist when he asserted that the kingdom of heaven is within, that there is nothing from without a man that entering into him can defile him, but the things which come out of him defile him. The oneness and the organic nature of the universe is what is made explicit by his synthesis of the real and the ideal nature of human experiences in the universe. God is within and also without. The world is within us and also without us. Asceticism and love are both our duties. A parallel integration of the interior and the exterior forces through spiritual regeneration would confirm the kingdom of God on earth. In the teachings of Christ a careful student finds wisdom and holiness, metaphysics and ethics, realism and idealism, self-withdrawal and self-expression, knowledge and its object, fused into one in a most wondrous and comprehensible manner.

Only a God-man can do it, and Christ was one such. His life is a precept, and his precept is the word of God, by hearing and following which the unending beatitude of man is made secure.

CHRIST'S DIVINE LIFE

(Sri Swami Chidananda)

Light of the World, my heart's adoration to Thee, Lord, and prostrations again and again in utter lowliness of spirit! Glory be to Thee for ever and for ever!

Lord Jesus the Christ IS; here and now! Christ is Eternal. He has proclaimed this truth to the world not so much by words but by His glorious Resurrection. Where then is He to be sought and found? He abides where Virtue is and goodness. He is enshrined in the Divine Life of Love, Purity, Truth, Holiness, Prayer, Ceaseless Service and utter selflessness. In the heart where shine the light of Faith, Devotion, Humility, calm resignation to the Divine Will, Compassion and a genuine thirst for Righteousness, therein is Christ present, vibrant, vitally alive and radiantly manifest. O beloved Brethren! be ye also like Jesus and you shall find Christ within yourself now.

Christ is to be lived by each of us. His glorious life is for the Being and the Doing of it in and through our self even as He was and as He did. Thomas á Kempis was one of those great souls who declared this important Law of the spiritual realm in unmistakable terms to the world. If you would obtain the Kingdom of Heaven of Light, Bliss and Immortality then you have to be Christ-like in your life and actions. The direct and clear declaration of the Saviour Himself is no less emphatic on this point; for we have it from His own blessed lips, "Not every one who saith Lord, Lord shall enter the Kingdom of Heaven; but he that doth the Will of my Father which is in Heaven." And this Will of the Divine Father is personified in the Divine Being of Jesus Christ. To imitate Christ, to follow Him, to mould ourselves in His image and to carry out every one of His sublime admonitions in our life and actions is to do the Will of the Father in the most complete and most effective way. If you sincerely wish to belong to Christ, to be one of the holy circle of His Own, this path is the only way, for the Lord has said, "He who doth the Will of God is my brother, my sister, my mother."

The greatest value, the real meaning and the deepest significance of Christ's LIFE to us is the Being and the Doing of IT, i.e., in your being as HE was and in your doing as HE did.

Christ has given Himself to Mankind not so much as a personality but as a way of living, as a Path. He embodies in Himself the method of the Divine Ascent. To rise from the little human personality you now possess and ascend into the Christ Consciousness is to ascend from the unreal to the Real, from darkness to Light Everlasting and from death to joyous Immortality. When you have the Christ Ideal before you as a shining example you cannot utter the excuse "Which is the way? I do not know the way. I would fain follow it if only I knew." The ringing assertion of Christ, "I am the Way, the Truth and the Life; no one comes to Father but by me." Yes, verily, verily is it true that growing into the Christ Ideal is the one sure and certain Key to the Kingdom of Immortality.

To bring about this transformation the Saviour has Himself given invaluable cues if only we will discern them from His words and deeds. Recall the incident of the cleaning of the Temple and the visit of the Saviour to the house of Zacchus the tax-gatherer in Jericho who resolved to atone for his past and to amply amend it by his changed mode of life. This then is the teaching, the true secret of spiritual transformation. First, cleanse thy inner nature thoroughly. Cleanse the temple of your heart of all base elements, all cruelty, deceit, bargaining spirit and worldliness. Make it a real house of God. This done, enter resolutely upon a changed course of life. Turn a new leaf completely. Salvation is yours for you have attained freedom from sin and thus qualified for immortality and eternal Bliss. This very Law of Spiritual Life, Christ expressed in a yet fuller and direct manner when he expounded the Sadhana to Necodemus the sincere Pharisee and again when he 'suffered little children to come unto Him' declaring, "Unless ye become like little children you cannot enter the Kingdom of Heaven." Yes you have to be born again and to become pure, innocent and egoless like little children. Then and then alone will the gates of the realm of radiant bliss swing open to you. But remember the change should be real, deep and complete. Not mere outward change in profession, superficial conduct. You must become a totally *"different person,"* an entirely *"new person!"* The old self must vanish in toto.

In His own simple Person Jesus typifies this sublime Child, the simple, pure, innocent and egoless child of the Father. His trust in the Father is complete. He is the 'beloved Son' in Whom the Father is 'well pleased'. To become like Him you have to FOLLOW HIM! This is the Call of the Christ-Spirit to Man. The Lord saith to us now, today even as He did in those blessed days to Philip of Bethsaida, the two thrilling Words, "FOLLOW ME." This is to be, not in the sense of the mere imitation of the superficial details of His life but in His ascent on the radiant inner Path of Goodness, Love, Compassion and utter self-effacement. And for those blessed ones who are prepared to 'Follow HIM' He has shown the Way by three *special* Commandments, firstly to the Pharisee who asks, "Master which is the greatest commandment in the Law?" and then through those memorable words, during those tragic last moments of His freedom as they walk up to the fateful garden of Gethsamane on the Mount of Olives. Saith the Lord, "God is one. Thou shalt love the Lord with *all thy heart, with all thy soul, with all thy mind and with all thy strength.*" And then, "THOU SHALT LOVE THY NEIGHBOUR AS THYSELF." The highest Vedantic Atma-bhava! And again, "I give you a new commandment that you love one another as I have loved you."

O humanity! what have you done to this priceless parting appeal of Jesus? O Men, O nations, O races where now is that Love Christ left to you as His sublime heritage? To what cruel region have you relegated that peerless treasure of His Love? From whence this heritage of hatred and rapine that you have fatally embraced in the blindness of your spirit? Ye have crucified the gentle Jesus in the Golgotha of your greed-filled hearts! Even as the helpless Jerusalem is the world today in rejecting the love and Grace of God. Shall this indeed be the fate of this fair earth? No! is the emphatic reply. For as long as there are even a handful of the faithful in this world, even a handful who would joyously FOLLOW HIM, so long Hope shines bright upon the horizon of Man's future. For through them will the Christ Spirit re-live and enlighten the earth. They will be the Resurrection of the spirit amidst modern mankind. Through the faithful few will the blessings of the Christ-Consciousness be showered upon mankind.

Christ is but His Teachings. He is embodied in His precepts. He who LIVES these precepts fulfills the main duty of his life, the sole purpose of his existence. Admiration, adoration and glorification of the Christ personality and Ideal, devoid of earnest, active, practical imitation will never, never do. The life of such a Great One is to be lived again by us. Thus and thus alone do you fulfil yourself in His Spirit.

May the World heed His Commandments, His Call! May one and all arise and FOLLOW HIM! May the Shepherd strengthen us and lead us safely from darkness and sorrow into eternal Light and Bliss Everlasting! Glory, glory be to Lord Jesus, the Christ. Amen.

THE CHRIST TO THE SPIRITUAL ASPIRANT

(Sri Swami Krishnananda)

Jesus the Christ, the Light of the world, the Supreme Logos made visible to the human eye, stands as an unparalleled example and pattern of sacrifice, love, knowledge and realisation of Truth. To the Sadhaka or the spiritual aspirant the person of Jesus reflects the art of the inner life, life in the spirit. Christ, the Son of Man, representing the life and voice of humanity and forming as it were the sum and substance of the essence of man, is the Son of God, the incarnate effulgence of the Sovereign of the Universe. It is the crystallisation of spirit that we call the Mystic Christ, the Light that is born to save the world of darkness. As the darkness of the world is not an outward phenomenon, so is the remover of this darkness not a mere physical personality. Great men are not seen from their bodies. It is not the form or the body that is the great man. The great man is the behaviour, the conduct, the character, the speech, the thought and conscious expression of any kind. From these special characteristics the presence of the great man is inferred and directly perceived. He is great who has comprehended that stupendous ocean of Spirit, the Great God that twinkles in all eyes, that resides in the hearts of all beings.

We have in Christ the great man of the Spirit, and his life is a picturesque drama of Adhyatmika Sadhana or spiritual living. From his manifestation to his re-absorption he displayed the magnificence of God and established His Glory on earth. When the spiritual child is about to be born the Ruler of the empire of darkness shall try to slay it and the child has to be protected with great difficulty. Once the child grows up it shall take care of itself. The individual person is the parent of the new-born spiritual boy and let him guard it against the onslaught of the Ego, the king of this city where the baby is born. Just at the time when the spiritual consciousness tries to emerge out by gradual steps a natural revolt of the unspiritual forces is quite inevitable. It is true that ghee is burnt up when it is poured into fire, but if a maund of ghee is poured over a spark of fire, the spark will be extinguished. When the spark becomes a huge conflagration any amount of ghee can be consumed by it. In like manner, the worldly tendencies would overpower the spiritual spark when it is in the infant stage, but the conflagration of spiritual consciousness shall burn up worldly tendencies and all evil. What is called the "dark night of the soul," in the terminology of the mystics, is a stage where the consciousness is smothered and is smouldering amidst the darkness of ignorance. The birth of Sri Krishna is involved in similar circumstances and is indicative of similar facts, and the first Chapter of the Bhagavadgita depicting the dejection of spirit of the aspiring soul marks identical situations. The spiritual self is bound to succeed, and destroy nescience root and branch.

The work of the manifesting Spirit is not complete even when it has begun to reep through the vesture of flesh, after managing to save itself from the attacks of the outward nature. The greater trouble arises from the higher planes of nature. Difficult enough it is, no doubt, to pass through the forest of the gross physical nature, but more difficult and hazardous is the attempt to overcome the subtler forces of the vibrant mental nature which is the pivot of outward universal activity. When the soul sheds sufficient light, enough to blind the eyes of the psychological nature, a revolt of the latter becomes the result. This revolt is now in no way advantageous to the lower nature; for it only means the revelation of the extraordinary power of spiritual knowledge and experience and the crucifixion of the flesh, the very playground of the lower nature. The individualistic vestment is cast off, the turbulent passionate nature is punished and the son of Man re-enters the Kingdom of God which is the birth-right of the son of God.

In Christ one finds the 'Jivanmukta' of the Indians. As one standing at noon in cool waters up to the waist experiences cold and heat simultaneously, the illumined sage moving on earth, with a body, experiences bliss and trouble simultaneously, with his head and heart in Heaven and feet on earth. Jesus came to make people understand and know in experience that the aim of life is not *to do* something else, but *to be* something else. It is not wrong action that should attract our attention and demand rectification, but the organic defect in us which is the source and the root of wrong action. Unless one is *reborn* there is no hope. To become something completely different, to change one's nature, to be initiated into the unique spiritual experience, means dying to the life of flesh and being alive to the superior awareness. It is not the ceremonial act of the Jew, but the consciousness-experience of the Christian that is the ultimate solace of the individual, that is at present confined to the narrow tabernacle which is the abode of all corruption and pain. It is not subjection to rule and rigidity of ritual that is the law of spirit, but perfect freedom in the Glory of God-consciousness. Man is the child of the Universe by birth, but he is the child of God by re-birth. Self-control and asceticism are the roads to inner peace. The pleasures of the world are vain, tantalising and deceitful; they are not worth being resorted to, He who loves the world loves not the Father.

Christ was conscious of Adhikaribheda among students of spiritual knowledge and was particular to impart the higher wisdom to the initiates alone, to those who are capable of rousing the inner consciousness, while to the outwardly busy he spoke in parables. "Unto you is given the mystery of the Kingdom of God; but unto them that are without, all things are done in parables." "And which many such parables spake he the word unto them, as they were able to hear it; and without a parable spake he not unto them: but privately to his own disciples he expounded all things." Jesus has clearly told his disciples that he had many other things which he wanted to speak to them but which they could not understand. Jesus comes close to Hindu and Buddhistic ideals in many respects, and sounds practically an echo of the ethical teaching of these older religions. The death or non-existence of the immediate personal existence is, to all these religions, the condition of the new richer life.

To merge in the satiating waters of immortality, one must first drink of the cup of death. No man on earth, generally speaking, is prepared for this order. This, too, is illustrated in the life of Jesus. He wished that the cup be taken away from him,—look at the force with which the lower nature presses the soul,—but he opened his eyes and his vision became clear, and he said: "Thy will be done." The stresses of physical life entangle the higher and nobler reaches of the soul, and to keep one's balance in the face of manifest hostility is indeed a tremendous task. It is given to a very few like Jesus to dive into the depths constantly and regain the solacing consciousness which is immaterial and trans-empirical. The whole life of Jesus is one tale of the march of the soul to its destination which is the complete unfolding of consciousness.

A life of mere negativity is not what is preached by Christ. It is not only the emptying of the soul, the selling away of whatever we have, the parting with everything that we possess, but the supreme fulfilment of Spirit through divine contemplation. But the rejection of the outward show is a necessary pre-condition of this divine fulfilment. We cannot fill a vessel with nectar when it already contains filth to the brim. Spiritual life is at once the transcending of the mundane consciousness and the saturation of oneself in the metempirical Self-consciousness or God-consciousness.

The student or aspirant who wishes to lead the life ideal should receive inspiration from the conduct of Jesus, from his life and teachings, live a life of holiness and piety, embrace humility and poverty, become a friend of the poor, love the neighbour as himself, sacrifice his all to Him, suffer and weep for His sake, cast off the flesh and its passions, and die to be born for the life eternal. It means the withdrawal of faith in things that seem and perish resting on the firm belief in the omnipotence of the Maker of all things, and caring not for oneself and one's needs, for God shall take care of all, with His simultaneous knowledge of past, present and future. This reborn soul is the sage, the Rishi, the Mukta, the redeemed one who is one with God. The son and the Father are one. The universe produces a rare ripe fruit of a saint from its fine flower of virtue and knowledge, makes him the cream of mankind and sacrifices him to the Great Father. Here is the consummation of existence. Christ's ascension to Heaven is regaining the Consciousness of God.

Christ was the matchless spiritual teacher who pointed out that the Kingdom of Heaven is within. All his other teachings are a commentary on this text. His teaching is summed up by his statement: "I and my Father are one." The individual soul is one with the Supreme Being. *Ayamatma Brahma. Sarvam Khalvidam Brahma. Jivo Brahmaiva Naaparah.*

OM TAT SAT

THE PROMISES OF JESUS

(Sri Sudarshan Sharma)

"Come unto me, all ye that labor,
And are heavy laden, and I will give rest."
(Matthew xi, 28)

". . . and him that cometh to me
I will in no wise cast out." (John vi, 36)

Here is an invitation from Jesus. It is so personal, so intimate and so warm. It bears the promise that will not fail. Heaven and earth shall pass away but his words shall not pass away for, the words are not of Jesus but HIS that sent him. He seeks not his own will but the will of the heavenly Father.

He extends this invitation to all those who are unhappy and full of unrest. Everyone, who is shaken cruelly by the rough hands of destiny, can look forward with hope, for courage and consolation. In fact it is just for such as are unhappy that Jesus came into this world. There are many whose life has been made bitter by sobs and sighs and who have lost interest in everything under the sun. They need not think themselves quite lost. There is much hope yet. They are not lonely and abandoned. There is some one who is deeply interested in their activities. His only aim is to complete that which is still unfulfilled. He would remove every thorn from the way and make the path straight if only they allow him to do so; if only they have faith in the saving power of Jesus. No one that has faith is quite lost. Alas for the human disbelief!

Jesus came not to criticise and reject but to accept and save man. This is the reason why he is known as the Saviour and not as the propounder of a system of abstract philosophy. This is also the reason why he placed love high above intellect. He knew that man does not live by the light of knowledge alone but needs the warmth of intimate love also. He needs to be understood, but more than that, he needs to be saved from the shafts of sorrow and adversity. Howsoever fallen the condition of a man may be, he would still like to live, and live in peace and happiness. Jesus knew it, and took upon himself the responsibility of showing the way. One would sometimes like to know why there is evil and suffering at all; and why one who is able to save us all, is not able to banish evil from earth. Why there is evil we do not know. We do not know whether evil as such would cease to be or not. But we do know that there is a way by which we can overcome evil, or at least minimise it, individually, and help others in overcoming it. As for the evil in general, it is a mystery. Perhaps it will always be there. Perhaps it is endemic to existence. As Jesus himself says:

"It must needs be that offences come." (Matthew xviii, 7)

"In the world ye shall have tribulation." (John xvii, 33)

What is of significance is not that there is evil but that there is a way to overcome it and that there is one who is very anxious to help us do so. This is enough.

The way consists in the teachings of Jesus. As a matter of fact the entire Gospel of the Kingdom of God is the way. We are not called upon to leave the world and join the Kingdom of God somewhere else, but to establish the Kingdom right here in our midst by good deeds. Good deeds depend on good motives. So, in the end, Kingdom of God is a sort of rebirth in terms of changed attitudes. It is an internal re-orientation of outlook. This is why Jesus said: "The Kingdom of God is within you." This changed outlook must manifest in changed deeds bearing fruit worthy of name. In the Kingdom of God there would be a spirit of service; there would be more cooperation than competition. Men shall be governed by the inner spirit and not merely by outer advantages. No one will suffer for want of help nor shall there be iniquity among men. The vision of Isaiah would be fulfilled. "The Lord shall judge between the nations, and shall reprove many peoples, and they shall beat their swords into ploughshares, and their spears into pruning hook: nation shall not lift up sword against nation, neither shall they learn war any more." (Isaiah ii, 4)

The present century man needs just this Gospel. Having been disillusioned and ruined by the recurring wars, famines and pestilences, he looks for inner faith to hold his own against the might of circumstance. The vast technological advancement of the present century has merely made life more complex. It has not been able to heal the inner wounds born of endless strife and limitless disorder. There is unfortunately a tendency among people to hold Science responsible for all these evils. It is a mistake. To decry Science is not to solve the problem. The blame is not outside but inside. Were men any the better when there was no scientific outlook? They behaved in much the same way. Doing away with Science will make us materially worse without making us spiritually better. And, after all, what is Science except a reasoned attitude towards men and things? What we need is a faith that will reawaken our belief in the worth of existence and value of moral life. Science is to be supplemented, not discarded. Science is not incompatible with religion.

In Jesus we find the faith, the way and the life. We must fulfil and not destroy even as Jesus did. We must have life and have it more abundantly. All life-preserving ideas are good. To preserve and promote life is to serve. To serve would mean, to take less and give more. All those who take upon themselves the cross of Jesus and serve, are called upon to inherit the Kingdom of God.

"For I was hungered, and ye gave me meat: I was thirsty, and ye gave me drink: I was a stranger, and ye took me in: naked, and ye clothed me: I was sick, and ye visited me: I was in prison, and ye came unto me." (Matthew xxx, 35-36)

This is the way of service. Everyone is called upon to do his best and do it timely. There is no time to lose. Jesus asks us to work

"While it is day for, the night cometh,
when no man can work." (John ix, 4)

Remember the work and remember also "the night." Do as much as you can. Do not fear difficulties and discomforts. If you remember Jesus and his works, he too will remember you and would readily come to your help. Remember his promise:

"I will not leave you comfortless: I will come to you." (John xiv, 18)

LIFE OF JESUS
FOR A SPIRITUAL ASPIRANT
(Swami Chidananda)

Blessed Satchidananda Atman,

"*Asato ma sat gamaya, tamaso ma jyotirgamaya, mrityorma amritam gamaya.*" "*Sarve bhavantu sukhinah, sarve santu niramayah, sarve bhadrani pasyantu, ma kaschit duhkhabhagbhavet.*"

In thus offering you my devout worship and adorations upon this most holy Christmas Day at the command of our divine Master, Satgurudev, I started with two Sanskrit prayers and it was with a particular purpose that I opened with these prayers. First I chanted "*Asato ma sat gamaya, tamaso ma jyotir gamaya, mrityor ma amritam gamaya.*" It means "From the unreal, lead us on to the Real. From darkness, lead us on to Eternal Light and from mortality, lead us on to Immortality" and then I followed up with the prayer for cosmic weal, wherein the prayer goes, "*Sarve bhavantu sukhinah, sarve santu niramayah.*" May all be happy. May all be free from diseases. "*Sarve bhadrani pasyantu, ma kaschit duhkhabhagbhavet.*" May welfare be unto all. May auspiciousness be unto all. May there be no sorrow to anyone."

It is precisely to bring about this state of universal happiness, goodwill and brotherhood amidst all mankind, and peace all over the earth, it is in order to bring about this state of affairs on earth and to elevate man from this earthly life into a divine life and a higher life of spiritual experience and spiritual realisation, that from time to time great souls who are the incarnated embodiments of the Supreme Divine Spirit, God, come down in the form of men. It is to do this that these great souls come upon the earth and through their lives, their activities and their example, and precepts, they teach man how to bring about these things, how each one can contribute to the sum total of goodness, to the sum total of welfare in the world, and how by living a life of goodness, auspiciousness, love and service, we can transform this life and attain immortality, how we can rise from this life of ignorance and untruth to perennial light and eternity. And the life of Christ is an example of such a lofty life of Lokasangraha, so that the whole of humanity may know the way to eternal existence. He taught us the way to divine perfection and this great soul incarnated upon the earth long, long ago, and because his great divine life was thus lived in order to bring about a transformation not only on the life upon earth but a transformation in the hearts of mankind,—it is because he did this work, the world has deified him and adores him even to this day. That is why even thousands of miles away we celebrate here the great Christmas. It is sacred to entire mankind, because Christ came to lead man from darkness to light, from mortality to immortality and from the life of clinging to unreality to a life established in Atmic consciousness.

He took birth in humble surroundings. He was born in a manger, a place where fodder for cattle was kept. He was born of a carpenter. It is as though to bring out the truth that the divine spirit takes birth in that being who is humble, who is pure, who is meek in spirit, in whom there is no pride, it is as though to symbolise this truth he was born in this humble inn, in a manger, and about his lofty life we can give countless sermons, yet we would not reach the limit of his glory and grandeur. But let us recall to our minds a few incidents in the life of Jesus and a few of the precious words that came out of his lips.

One of the parables taught by Jesus is the parable of the sower. The seed that is sown on a rock does not sprout. The seed which is sown on thorns gets choked up and it does not grow.

The seed which is sown on a fertile soil sprouts and grows well. It is the ground that makes the seed fruitful. Even so, unless we make the ground of our hearts suitable by acquiring the necessary qualifications, by becoming pure, by generating faith and devotion, unless we do that, all the divine scriptures, all the saints will not be able to do much for us. At least this part of making ourselves suitable vessels, is a thing which is incumbent upon a Sadhaka. Therefore, he who aspires for spiritual realisation, let him remember the parable of the sower and the seeds and try to make himself a fit receptacle for the seeds of spirituality. Only if we do that our life will be fruitful.

Secondly, a beautiful parable that Christ has given which shows the way to the Kingdom of Heaven. It is the parable of Good Samaritan. Our love should not be coloured by selfishness. Christ said, "Love thy neighbour as thyself," and one man asks him, "Who is a neighbour"? He does not answer the question in a direct way, but gives a parable of the good Samaritan and asks the person who put him the question, "Who is the neighbour?" It is the heart full of love, worshipfulness, that determines who is the neighbour. Worshipfulness should be active, purposeful, practical. A man who was an enemy of a person was injured by the robbers, then the man who was supposed to be an enemy, showed the unity of heart actively and practically and showed that he was the real neighbour. And that man had to come to the Kingdom of Heaven, because he had enshrined within himself the same love which indwelt Christ and which made him give up his body upon the cross. That love which made Christ suffer for the sake of people who had never seen him, that love which made Christ wear the crown of thorns that brought blood out of his body, that love is the key to Christ Consciousness and Immortality.

And last, but not least, once again Lord gives us the lofty parable of the virgins with the lamps. It is not a parable which is remembered by all, but it has got a great significance, especially to us, seekers, who are trying to tread the path of Yoga, which is doubtless a hard path, which is a path meant for those alone who have a heart that has got undying faith. The strength of the devotee is not the strength of the muscle, but the strength of faith. Even if the whole solar system will crash and crumble, once he has grasped the hand of the Lord, the Lord will not forsake him. This strength is necessary for our path. I said the story of the virgins to point out how careful we have to be in order to take full advantage of our existence. There were seven virgins. They were waiting for the Lord who was to come. They waited and waited with lamps with them and it became dark, and the Lord did not come. The virgins became sleepy and they fell asleep. They did not take care to replenish the oil in the lamps or to trim the wick. But there was one among them who was very careful. She was very sincere to unite with the Lord. Sincerity is the secret of Yogic life. Other people cannot tell us whether our aspiration is keen enough or not. But sincerely and without partiality we have to find out whether sincerity is there or not. That virgin was ever awake. She was careful, and she trimmed the wick, replenished the lamp with oil and lo! when all other virgins were sleeping, and darkness had come, at that moment, Christ appeared and when He came, one was awake, and he took her unto himself and eternally the soul was united with the oversoul, which is the fruition of Yoga. Blessedness and bliss accrued to that soul. What about others? They never knew when the Lord came. They lamented when they woke up, but their lamentation was of no use. And what does Gurudev tell us? He tells us the same parable. He tells us more forcibly. He says, "Life is short, time is fleeting. Awake, arise and attain the goal. Keep yourself ever ready to meet the Lord. Be up and doing in Yogic Sadhana." Let not a moment pass without effort to reach God. Let us be not like the virgins who fell asleep, but like the virgin who was awake and vigilant and who trimmed the wick, and attained oneness with the Lord.

Above all, what is the greatest parable that Jesus has taught. Even as Swamiji has preached it, there is one greatest sermon that Christ preached. What is it? His own personal life. How he reacted to his surroundings, what was his purity, what was his wonderful compassion, what was his humility? He was an embodiment of all the gospels that he has given, only in a thousandfold increased measure. The inspiration of that great example is a perennial and living lesson to all of us to keep before our eyes. It is the star that we have to follow. There is no darkness as long as we keep our eyes fixed on the star. By following that star, both men of wisdom and men of faith reach the very abode of Lord. If we keep our eyes fixed upon the great Light which is Jesus, we shall surely attain the Lord, with the blessings of all saints.

Let this be our resolve on this great day that we shall follow the star and attain the Lord.

May God bless you all.

A SIGNIFICANT CHAPTER IN THE BIBLE

(Sri Swami Sivananda)

One of my favourite chapters in the Bible is in the First Epistle of Paul, the Apostle, the Corinthians, which I quote below, giving my reasons for liking it.

"Though I speak with the tongues of men and of angels, and have not charity, I am become as sounding brass, or tinkling cymbal.

"And though I have the gift of prophecy, and understand all mysteries, and all knowledge; and though I have all faith so that I could remove mountains, and have not charity, I am nothing.

"And though I bestow all my goods to feed the poor and though I give my body to be burned, and have not charity, it profiteth me nothing.

"Charity suffereth long, and is kind; charity envieth not; charity vaunteth not itself, is not puffed up, doth not behave itself unseemly, seeketh not her own, is not easily provoked, thinketh no evil, rejoiceth not in iniquity, but rejoiceth in the truth; beareth all things, believeth all things, hopeth all things, endureth all things.

"Charity never faileth: but whether there be prophecies, they shall fail; whether there be tongues, they shall cease; whether there be knowledge, it shall vanish away.

"For we know in part, and we prophesy in part. But when that which is perfect is come, then that which is in part shall be done away.

"When I was a child, I spake as a child, I understood as a child, I thought as a child; but when I became a man, I put away childish things. For now we see through a glass darkly; but then face to face, now I know in part; but then shall I know even as also I am known.

"And now abideth faith, hope, charity, these three; but the greatest of these is charity."

I love this chapter very much, because it is not only poetic and beautiful, but seems to me to portray such a perfect picture of the qualities of our Lord Jesus Christ. And also, it contains a promise.

In the opening sentences, we are told of the utter uselessness of all other spiritual qualifications, unless we possess the one and the most redeeming quality of charity. Charity covers a wide range of virtues—selflessness, surrender of egoism, fellowship, amity, forgiveness, compassion and, above all, pure love.

We are told that a person of charity must be patient, humble, unselfish, honest, constant, kind, and absolutely pure.

And then, finally, we are given a promise, a promise that we shall eventually be brought "face to face" with our Lord.

The two salient virtues which stand out most clearly in my mind when I read this passage, are those of kindness and purity. And perhaps next to these I would put constancy; the constancy of love, the love that never fails. Love is kind. To be loving we must be kind. Surely kindness is of the very essence of love. To be kind is to be compassionate and forgiving; to be kind is to try not to hurt others' feelings; to be kind is to be gentle and sweet; to be kind is to be sympathetic and understanding, and ready to help a friend in need. It is not only the positive things we do and say and think that constitute kindness, but it is often the things we do not do or say or think. How often we can be kind by not passing on that unkind remark we hear about a friend, or by not saying that thoughtless and tactless word that is on the tip of our tongue.

And, then, we have purity. Charity "thinketh no evil." What absolute purity, to think no evil at all, not even a single evil thought; how divinely pure, and yet this was indeed the blessed state of our Lord Jesus Christ. We are told to love the Lord our God with all our heart and all our soul, through all our days; and to do this, we should not only act in a pure way, but we must have pure thoughts, always. We must attribute nothing but the best motives to other people; our every thought must be holy and unselfish and in accordance with God's Will. What a glorious ideal!

And, then, we are told of the constancy—"charity never faileth." Charity never lets you down; he who truly loves you, never lets you down, and if we love others, we should never let them down. Our Lord's love for us was constant and never failed us, and his love is still constant and with us today. It is the one thing we can completely rely upon. And so we see that true love is loyal, devoted, constant, and never fails.

Finally, we come to the promise. First we are told we must have faith; we must believe; next we must have hope, we must want fulfilment of the thing in which we believe; and, finally, we have a promise. Here is the assurance of complete fulfilment of that for which we hope. "For now we see through a glass darkly, but then face to face." All our doubts will be cleared, all the things we do not understand will be made plain to us, all the clouds of darkness will be swept away; there will be no more separation from God but all will be absolute unity and clarity, for then we shall be "face to face."

And so, to sum up, I love this 13th chapter of the Epistle to the Corinthians, not only because of its poetic beauty, and the glory of the promise in the closing verse, but I love it for the beautiful picture I see portrayed of our Lord Jesus Christ as epitomised in charity and love, the essential qualities of which, to me, are those of constancy, purity and kindness.